EXAM REVISION

AS/A-LEVEL

Business Studies

2nd Edition

Malcolm Surridge

Philip Allan Updates
Market Place
Deddington
Oxfordshire
OX15 0SE

tel: 01869 338652
fax: 01869 337590
e-mail: sales@philipallan.co.uk
www.philipallan.co.uk

ISBN 0 86003 439 9

Printed by Raithby, Lawrence & Co Ltd, Leicester

Contents

Chapter 4 Operations management

Chapter 5 External influences

Chapter 6 Objectives and strategy

Introduction

About this book

This book of revision notes is intended to form a central part of your revision programme. Read this introduction carefully before you attempt to use the notes that follow. There is some important advice which is intended to help you improve your performance and final grade.

These notes cover all the important subject matter that may be taught as part of the AS and A-level Business Studies course. The content and the examination advice have been fully revised to take into account the changes introduced in 2003. Thus you can use the book with confidence.

Topics that are covered by particular examination boards are shown in the chart on pages 202–206. This will help you to identify *exactly* what is on your particular specification and to make sure you study only relevant topics. However, specifications are updated regularly, so it is important that you check for any changes. Having an up-to-date copy of your particular specification, and ticking off topics as you revise them, will help you to prepare for your AS and A-level examinations.

The book is divided into six chapters relating to the modules that commonly comprise A-level Business Studies, namely **marketing**, **accounting and finance**, **people and organisations**, **operations management**, **external influences** and **objectives and strategy**. In turn each of these chapters is divided up into two sections, AS and A2. This will assist you in revising the relevant material.

However, the three main awarding bodies that offer AS and A-level Business Studies (AQA, Edexcel and OCR) have not all split the material between AS and A2 in the same ways. In this book, the material is divided according to the AQA specification, as the largest number of students take this examination. The chart on pages 202–206 highlights where differences occur in the specifications and especially those topics that might be included within AS or A2 sections, depending on the awarding body. If you are taking Edexcel or OCR examinations, you should look carefully at this.

For AS examinations you will only need to revise the AS sections. No questions will be set on A2 topics. However, for A2 examinations you are advised to **revise AS as well as A2 materials**. While A2 examinations are unlikely to set questions on topics that are part of the AS specification, it may be helpful to draw on AS information. For example, an A2 question on marketing strategy is likely to require you to draw on some AS knowledge, such as the marketing mix.

Make sure you are clear which sections of the book relate to the topics you are studying at any given time and work through the relevant chapter. This will:
- identify any material that you may not have covered
- reinforce your initial learning
- provide a sound basis for revision prior to the examination(s)

How to revise for AS/A-level Business Studies examinations

- The most important thing about preparing for examinations in AS and A-level Business Studies is to **plan well ahead**.
- **Note down the dates of your examinations.** All Business Studies courses have modular examinations, i.e. exams on the individual modules comprising the course. These modular examinations take place in January and June of each year. This means that you might face three or four series of examinations as part of your entire A-level Business Studies course.
- Make sure you know exactly **what material you need to revise for the examination and the style of the examination**. Does the exam take the form of a case study (either pre-issued or issued on the day), data-response question(s), an essay, a business report or a combination of these? You should plan a full programme of revision well ahead of any examinations you may be taking.
- **Plan your revision carefully.** If you do not like a section of the specification, make sure you revise it early so that you can iron out any problems — perhaps with help from your teacher or lecturer. He or she will also be able to comment on your revision plans.
- **Look at past papers.** You should have a complete set of past papers. They are invaluable for examination practice. They allow you to see topics that have been examined recently and those not tested for some time. They also enable you to familiarise yourself with the style and level of question that you will encounter on the day of the examination. These should play a greater role in the later stages of your revision programme. You need to have mastered the subject matter before you start practising past questions. It is also helpful to get hold of copies of at least some of the associated marking schemes. These will allow you to see the sorts of answer that examiners were anticipating to each question and the types of examination skill that you were expected to use.
- **Use these Exam Revision Notes as the centrepiece of your revision.** This book will provide you with all the basic information you require. Do not hesitate to write in the book. Tick off subjects as you feel confident about them. Highlight those topics you find difficult and look at them in detail, using your class notes and textbook to support your study.
- **Make sure that you cover all the topics that may form a part of the examination.** Do not skip topics. Plan your revision programme so that you can work steadily through all the topics in the weeks leading up to the examination. Do not be too ambitious as to how much you can do each week. This means you have to start in plenty of time. This is particularly true if you are revising for several AS or A-level examinations in the same sitting.
- **Take any tips on revision techniques from teachers and friends, but do what works for you.** You might find that you remember topics and interrelationships (e.g. the consequences of high gearing) by drawing spider diagrams. On the other hand, you may benefit from completing lots of past papers.
- Everyone revises differently. **Find out what routine suits you best**: alone or with a friend; in the morning or late at night; in short, sharp bursts or in longer revision sessions. Whatever approach you adopt, build in breaks to ensure you remain fresh.
- **Raise any problems or areas of difficulty with your teacher or lecturer** — it is important to eliminate areas of misunderstanding.
- **Attend any revision classes put on by your teacher or lecturer** — remember, he or she is an expert at preparing people for examinations.

DON'Ts

- **Don't** leave your revision to the last minute.
- **Don't** avoid revising subjects you dislike or find difficult — in fact, do them first.
- **Don't** forget that there is a life beyond revision and exams — build leisure and relaxation into your revision programme.
- **Don't** cram all night before an exam. You would be better to have a night away from revision.

On the day of the examination

- Have a good breakfast.
- Make sure you know where the exam is being held.
- Give yourself plenty of time to get there.
- Take everything you need — extra pens, water, tissues, a watch, Polo mints!
- If you feel anxious, breathe slowly and deeply to help you to relax.

In the examination room

- **Read the instructions at the top of the exam paper and follow them carefully**: a surprising number of students attempt three questions when they have been asked to answer two, for example. Others attempt all the questions, rather than the specified number. Make sure you do not do this.
- **Skim over the paper**, identifying the question areas you have revised for. Spot the questions you can do. Read them carefully.
- **Manage your time carefully**. Most A-level Business Studies examinations state the number of marks given for each element of a question. Prior to entering the exam room, you should have worked out how much time you have to answer each part of a question according to the mark allocation — read the examiner's tip below.

Examiner's tip

The best way to manage your time is to calculate the ratio between marks on the paper and the time allocation for the entire paper. This ratio can then be applied throughout the paper, so ensuring that you have time to answer all the questions you should.

Example

Suppose your Business Studies examination lasts for 90 minutes and the paper is worth 80 marks. If you assume that you will spend 10 minutes reading the paper, this leaves you 80 minutes to plan and write your answers. You therefore have 80 minutes to answer questions worth 80 marks. This means you can afford to spend 1 minute on a question for each mark allocated to it. In these circumstances, you should spend 10 minutes on a 10-mark question and 2 minutes on a 2-mark question.

- **Read through the paper carefully**, especially if you have to make a choice of questions. It is vital that you are clear about what the questions are asking and, if you have to make a choice, that you choose those questions on which you can perform best.
- **Jot down answer plans** before you tackle a question. Only begin writing when you have a clear idea of what the question calls for and your response. Be prepared to amend

your answer plan as you develop your answer. Other ideas and information will come to mind as you write; note them in your plan before you forget them.

- In planning your answers, **ensure you know what examination skills are required**. Some questions simply require knowledge; others call for analysis and/or evaluation (see 'Assessment objectives in A-level Business Studies' below). The command word and the mark allocation will tell you what is required.
- As you write your responses, **glance occasionally at the question** you are answering. This will help you to write relevantly.
- You may find it reassuring to **attempt your best question first** to settle your nerves. However, do make sure that the questions are not sequential, with the responses to later questions depending on your earlier answers.
- **If you are stuck on a question, go on to the next.** You can always come back to the unfinished one later.
- **Presentation is important.** Set your work out neatly using plenty of paragraphs. A new paragraph is invaluable to indicate a new aspect of the question, or that you are using a new examination skill.
- This also applies to **numerical questions**. Set your work out clearly, spacing it out and showing all relevant calculations. Key figures within your answers should be labelled to assist the examiner. In this way, you will receive credit for your work even if you make an arithmetical error.
- **Stay strictly within the time constraints you have calculated.** It is important that you attempt all the questions in order to maximise your marks.
- **Once the exam is over, relax.** Don't brood over any problems in an exam that is completed. It is better to concentrate on the next examination and then to relax when they are all over.
- **Pace yourself during the examination period.** Following a tough examination, a couple of hours spent with friends or watching television will do you more good than a further session of revision.

Examiner's tips

(1) Ask your teacher or tutor about tips on how to revise, and also about exam skills.

(2) Take short rests during your time of work and revision. If your mind is tired, you will find it difficult to take anything in.

(3) Plan your work: revise at times when you know you will work at your best.

(4) Start your revision early — this will help to avoid stress.

(5) Exercise: you need exercise to work well. Walk, run, play sport — whatever you enjoy most.

(6) Practise past questions to confirm subject knowledge and develop appropriate examination skills.

(7) Plan your time carefully in the examination.

(8) Talk to teachers and friends during your revision period — do not shut yourself away completely.

(9) Relax immediately before an examination to avoid being too tired on the day.

(10) Be sensible: if it upsets you to talk to your friends about an exam when it is over, don't do it. In fact, don't even think about the exam you have finished.

Assessment objectives in A-level Business Studies

You may ask: 'what are assessment objectives'? They are skills you require if you are to succeed in A-level Business Studies, or any other A-level examination for that matter. We have already seen that you will need *understanding* of the subject matter as set out in the specification, but this is not sufficient for success at A-level. You must also have examination skills, such as being able to *apply* your knowledge to the scenario, and to write *analytically* and *evaluatively*. One of the most important formulae to learn for A-level is:

A-level success = subject knowledge + examination skills

Assessment objectives, or examination skills, in A-level Business Studies include:
- knowledge and critical understanding
- application of knowledge to unfamiliar situations
- analysis of problems, issues and situations
- collecting, collating, organising and presenting information
- evaluation and synopsis

You will see from this list that knowledge of business studies is only one of a number of skills necessary for success. A critical element of your revision will be to develop these skills. While analysis and evaluation are generally regarded as the key to high grades in A-level Business Studies, application is a skill that students find difficulty in mastering. To assist you in developing the skill of application, this second edition of *Exam Revision Notes* includes a feature entitled **Ideas for application**. This feature highlights topics where application may be important and gives some suggestions on ways to apply the theory. This feature is intended not to cover all possible scenarios or topics, but merely to encourage you to think in the right way. It is important to practise these skills through regular attempts at recent past papers.

Throughout these notes, headings are weighted. Each of the six chapters is subdivided as follows:

Main headings	A	B	C
Subdivided	1	2	3
Subdivided again	1.1	1.2	1.3
Subdivided yet again	1.1a	1.1b	1.1c

Within the text, important terms are emboldened to attract your attention. Finally, the 'Examiner's tips' throughout these notes are special pieces of advice written to help you to understand both the subject and how best to approach it. Good luck with your revision.

Acknowledgements

I would like to thank a number of people for their help in writing this book and in developing it into a second edition. Stuart Merrills offered some particularly valuable advice on the accounting and finance chapter and assisted in ironing out a number of errors in the numbers. I am most grateful to Philip Cross and Penny Fisher at Philip Allan Updates for suggesting the project and for their patient support in seeing the first and second editions through to publication. Lastly, I am indebted to Jackie for her tolerance, support and love.

Malcolm Surridge
April 2003

CHAPTER 1 Marketing

This chapter covers the essential elements of marketing within the AS and A-level specifications. As with all of the chapters, this is divided into two sections: AS marketing followed by A2 marketing. This division is based on the AQA specification, but you can use the chart on pages 202–206 to find out any differences in the specifications, including how OCR and Edexcel classify topics as AS or A2.

AS Marketing

This section considers the importance of the marketing function and looks in detail at market analysis, marketing strategy and marketing planning. Considerable emphasis is placed on the marketing mix to ensure understanding of the important techniques and principles that come under this heading.

A Introduction

1 Definitions

A number of definitions exist. According to the Chartered Institute of Marketing, marketing is defined as:

'...the management process which identifies, anticipates and supplies customer requirements efficiently and profitably'.

A wider definition is:

'Marketing is the human activity directed at satisfying needs and wants through the exchange process.'

Marketing involves a wide range of activities within businesses, including:

- research
- design
- testing
- quality control and assurance
- pricing

- advertising
- promotion
- distribution
- packaging
- after-sales service

Following the lead of Japanese businesses, many companies have disbanded their marketing departments, recognising that marketing affects everyone in the firm, from receptionists and shop-floor workers, to engineers, managers and directors.

2 The role of marketing in business

Marketing has a number of functions within a business. It collects and analyses data on markets and consumer behaviour. Once analysed, this information can be used to guide businesses as to the products they should produce and the best methods to promote them.

It encourages planning and target setting and the use of a more scientific approach to management and decision making. Furthermore, it encourages a business to be outward looking: to assess the actions and activities of rivals, pressure groups, governments and consumers, for example.

Some would argue that marketing should be the guiding philosophy for all the activities of a business. According to Peter Drucker: 'there is only one valid definition of business purpose: to create a customer'.

Businesses develop a marketing plan and a strategy to carry this out. A business that recognises the crucial role of marketing will assess the effectiveness of its plans regularly and adjust both plans and strategies to meet the needs of its customers. This process is summarised in Figure 1.1.

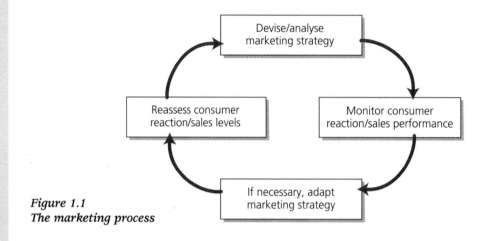

Figure 1.1
The marketing process

B Marketing strategy

Strategy is the medium- to long-term plan required to achieve a business's overall goals. The marketing strategy is merely the contribution made by the marketing department.

Developing a marketing strategy requires:
● careful analysis of the firm's current position
● complete understanding of the business and the market in which it operates
● some assessment of the resources available to the business

1 Marketing objectives

Marketing strategy entails the **setting of marketing objectives**. Marketing objectives are medium- to long-term targets that may provide a sense of direction to the marketing department and to the whole business. This is especially true if the targets are quantified. A business might set a **range of marketing objectives**, including the following:
● **To increase or maintain market share.** For example, a company might seek to increase market share (as measured by value of sales) from 20% to 25% over the next 3 years. Alternatively, it may decide to introduce a new product to maintain its current market share. For example, Mercedes introduced a small car to protect itself from increasing competition in the luxury car market.

- **To broaden its range of products to improve its market standing.** It may adopt an asset-led approach by using an existing brand name to develop new products. The Virgin Group is a classic example of such an approach.
- **To break into a new market (or market segment).** Kellogg's, for example, has marketed its breakfast cereals as a product that can be eaten at any time of the day.

The precise marketing objectives a firm might set will depend upon the size and type of firm, its position in the market and the nature and expected responses of competitors. Market research will also shape the marketing objectives set by a business.

Examiner's tip

This is a topic on which you could be required to write evaluatively. The marketing objectives set by a business depend upon the type of factors listed above. The key point is that we cannot say with certainty what objectives a firm might set. We need to consider the circumstances of the business and the environment in which it operates.

2 Niche and mass marketing

Niche marketing is **a corporate strategy based on identifying and satisfying small segments of a market**. Famous examples include Tie Rack and the radio station Classic FM. The advantages and disadvantages of niche marketing are as follows:

- The first company to identify a niche market can often gain a dominant market position as consumers become loyal to the product — even if its price is higher.
- Niche markets can be highly profitable, as companies operating in them often have the opportunity to charge premium prices.
- Because sales may be relatively low, firms operating in niche markets may not be able to spread fixed overheads over sufficient sales to attain acceptable profit margins.
- If a niche market proves to be profitable, it is likely to attract new competition, making it less attractive to the companies that first discovered the market.

Mass marketing occurs when **businesses aim their products at most of the available market.** For example, the Ford Focus is the UK's most popular car and is sold in a mass market. In contrast, Lotus sports cars are aimed at a niche market. Businesses must be able to produce on a large scale if they are to sell successfully in a mass market. This may mean that the firm has to invest heavily in resources such as buildings, machinery and vehicles. Often firms have to be price competitive to flourish in mass markets.

Ideas for application

A move to mass marketing is more likely to succeed if a business is producing a product with a wide appeal or one for which marketing might be used to develop this widespread appeal. Consider how firms supplying mobile phone services moved from a niche market (business purchasers) to a mass market.

However, firms supplying mass markets frequently produce large numbers of similar, standardised products, making production easier. They can also benefit from economies of scale, enhancing profitability.

Examiner's tip

This is a common topic for examination questions. Examiners frequently ask whether a move into a niche market, or from a niche to a mass market, is a wise strategy. You should consider the type of market and the type of firm in developing your answer and make sure you apply your response to the scenario throughout your answer.

3 *Other marketing strategies*

Firms can adopt other marketing strategies. Igor Ansoff, a writer on management, identified four other strategies.

- **Market development.** This is a relatively simple, low-risk strategy in that a business sells its existing product in a new market. For example, Manchester United has opened club shops in China, hoping to sell its existing products in a new, and very large, market.
- **Market penetration.** By adopting this strategy a business attempts to gain a greater share of its existing market. Mobile telephone service suppliers such as Orange and Vodafone attempt to increase their share of the market, which is no longer growing.
- **New product development.** As the name suggests, this strategy entails introducing new products into an existing market. Virgin uses this strategy extensively, as with its decision to offer financial services such as bank accounts.
- **Diversification.** When a firm introduces a new product into a new market, it is diversifying. This is potentially a risky strategy, as the firm is introducing a new product into a market about which it may know little. Virgin's decision to sell mobile telephone services in the USA is an example of diversification.

4 *Adding value*

Adding value is **the process of increasing the worth or value of some resources by working on them.** Thus the value of a newly manufactured car is greater than the raw materials that were put into it. The process of motor manufacturing has added value. Firms normally seek to maximise added value, either by minimising costs or by selling for the highest possible price. Some breweries add value to their products by creating theme pubs, enabling them to charge high prices for their products (beer, other drinks and meals), as consumers consider them to be of higher value.

Businesses commonly add value by creating a unique selling point or proposition (USP) for their products. A USP allows a business to differentiate its products from others in the market. This can help the business to develop advertising campaigns, assists in encouraging brand loyalty and may result in the firm charging a premium price. British Bakeries differentiates its Hovis 'Best of Both' bread as looking and tasting like white bread while possessing the nutritional advantages of brown bread.

5 *Developing a strategy for products*

5.1 The product life cycle

The product life cycle is the theory that all products follow a similar pattern throughout their life. The five stages are: development, introduction, growth, maturity, decline.

Products take varying amounts of time to pass through these stages. The Mars bar was launched in the 1920s and is still going strong. In contrast, the entire sales life span of Virtual Pets was about 2 years, while modern motor cars are expected to have a life cycle of about 10 years. The five stages are outlined below and illustrated in Figure 1.2.

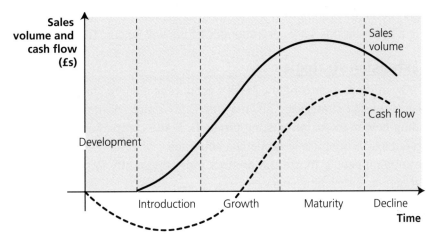

Figure 1.2 The product life cycle

(1) Development. Firms undertake research and development to create new products that will be their future best sellers. Many products fall by the wayside, as they do not meet the demands of consumers. This can be a very expensive stage, especially for firms operating in industries such as pharmaceuticals and electronic engineering. Cash flow is expected to be negative at this stage of a product's life.

(2) Introduction. This stage commences with the product's initial appearance on the market. At this time, sales are zero and the product has a negative cash flow. As time passes, sales should begin to rise, providing the company with some revenue. However, costs will remain high. The failure rate for new products is quite high, ranging from 60% to 90%, depending upon the industry. When a product is ready to be launched, the seller must ensure that potential buyers are aware of the new product. This can be very expensive and cash flow will remain negative. The price may have to be high to recoup the high initial costs of launching the product. For these reasons, many products never pass this stage.

(3) Growth. During the growth stage, sales rise rapidly and a firm's cash flow can improve considerably. The business's profits per unit sold are likely to be at a maximum. This is because firms tend to charge a high price at this stage, particularly if the product is innovatory. Firms with a technically superior good may well engage in **price skimming**. The growth stage is critical to a product's survival. The product's success will depend upon how competitors react to it. Profits per product can fall as more competitors enter the market and drive the price down while creating the need for heavy promotional expenditure by the original firm. At this point, a typical marketing strategy encourages strong brand loyalty to fight off the new competition.

(4) Maturity. During the maturity stage, the sales curve peaks and begins to decline. Both cash flow and profits also decline. This stage is characterised by severe competition with many brands in the market. Competitors emphasise improvements and differences in their versions of the product. Producers who remain in the market must make fresh promotional and distribution efforts. These efforts must focus on dealers as much as consumers to ensure that the product remains visible to the public. At this stage, consumers of the product know a lot about it and require specialist deals to attract their interest.

(5) Decline. During the decline stage, sales fall rapidly. New technology or a new product change may cause product sales to decline sharply. When this happens, marketing managers consider pruning items from the product line to eliminate those which are not earning a profit. At this stage, promotional efforts will be cut too.

5.2 Extension strategies

Firms may attempt to prolong the life of a product as it enters the decline stage by implementing extension strategies. They may use one or more of the following techniques:

- **Finding new markets for existing products.** Some companies selling baby milk have targeted less economically developed countries.
- **Encouraging people to use the product more frequently.** Breakfast cereals are often promoted as an evening snack.
- **Changing the appearance or packaging.** Some motor manufacturers have produced old models of cars with new colours or other features to extend the lives of their products.

Ideas for application

Extension strategies are more likely when new products take a considerable time to develop, as with cars. Extension strategies might also be more common in circumstances where managers have not handled the product portfolio effectively: for example, by not allocating sufficient funds to research and development.

Examiner's tip

For all major theories, such as the product life cycle, you should be able to give some assessment of the theory's strengths and weaknesses. This will help you to write evaluatively as well as confirming your understanding. An advantage of the life cycle might be that it helps a firm to plan (and finance) new products. Weaknesses might centre on the fact that different products are likely to have very different life cycles. A slump in sales might be due to external factors rather than the product entering its decline stage.

5.3 The product mix and the product portfolio

The product life cycle highlights that, in spite of extension strategies, products have finite lives of varying length. A well-organised business will plan its product range so that it has products in each of the major stages of the life cycle: as one product reaches decline, replacements are entering the growth and maturity stages of their lives (see Figure 1.3). This means that there will be a constant flow of income from products in the mature phase of their lives to finance the development of new products.

Firms can achieve this goal in two ways:

- **Product line policy** — extending the product line by producing variants on existing products. Nestlé, for example, has produced a white chocolate Kit Kat to extend its product range.
- **Product mix policy** — developing new products. For example, Volkswagen has introduced a new small car, the Lupo.

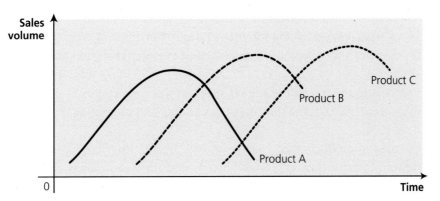

Figure 1.3 A healthy product mix

A number of tools are available to aid marketing managers in planning their product mix and strategy. One of the best known of these techniques is the **Boston matrix** produced by the Boston Consulting Group. The matrix allows businesses to undertake product portfolio analysis and is based on the premise that a product's market growth rate and its market share are important considerations in determining the marketing strategy.

The matrix, as shown in Figures 1.4 and 1.5, places products into four categories:

(1) **Star products** have a dominant share of the market and good prospects for growth.

(2) **Cash cows** are products with a dominant share of the market but low prospects for growth.

(3) **Dogs** have a low share of the market and no prospects for growth.

(4) **Problem children** are products that have a small share of a growing market and generally require a lot of funds to fulfil their potential.

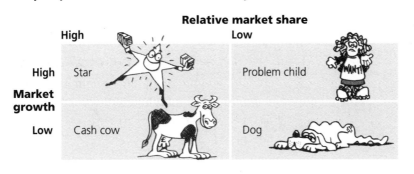

Figure 1.4 The Boston matrix

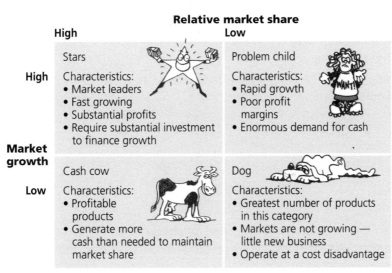

Figure 1.5 Features of the components of the marketing mix

A number of conclusions can be drawn from the Boston matrix:

- Firms should avoid having too many products in any single category. Obviously, firms do not want lots of dogs, but they also need to avoid having too many stars and problem children.
- Products in the top half of the chart are in the early stages of their life cycle and are in growing markets, but the cost of developing and promoting them will not have been recovered.
- Continuing production of cash cows will provide the necessary cash to develop the newer products. Cash cows will have passed the development stage, will have recovered their initial costs and will not require high promotional expenditure.
- Firms need problem child products as they may become tomorrow's cash cows.

C Analysing the market

1 Market research

Market research is the process of gathering data on potential consumers. This research can provide information on the buying habits, lifestyle and perceptions of actual and potential consumers.

1.1 Types of market research

Several different types of research may be undertaken by a business:

1.1a Market research
- analysis of market potential for existing products
- forecasting likely demand for new products
- sales forecasting for all products
- study of market trends
- study of market characteristics
- analysis of market shares

1.1b Product research
- customer acceptance of proposed new products
- comparative studies between competitive products
- studies into packaging and design
- forecasting new uses for existing products
- test marketing

1.1c Price research
- analysis of elasticities of demand
- analysis of costs and contribution or profit margin
- customer perceptions of price and quality
- the effects of changes in credit policy upon demand

Research can also be carried out into **sales promotion** (does advertising succeed?) and **distribution** (how does the firm get its products to the customer and where is it best to sell those products?).

1.2 Methods of market research

Understanding market research requires some definitions to be clear at the outset:

- **Primary data** — information that does not already exist. It is collected for a specific purpose by a market research agency or a business. It can be expensive and time consuming to collect, but should be accurate and precisely what the firm requires, possibly offering a competitive advantage.
- **Secondary data** — second-hand information gathered by someone else for another purpose at another time. Examples include government statistics and market intelligence reports. Such data are relatively cheap to gather, but might be out of date or fail to answer the questions the firm wishes to pose.

1.3 Field research

Primary data are normally collected through field research, which entails asking consumers questions directly. A number of techniques can be used to collect these data:

- **Surveys.** These can take a variety of forms. They may be based on a face-to-face interview and a questionnaire, possibly in the high street or in a retail outlet, or they may be conducted by telephone or by post.
- **Observation.** This involves watching people in a variety of circumstances. It can provide information on how consumers might react to in-store displays, prices or the location of products.
- **Loyalty cards.** These have been introduced comparatively recently. Although one function of loyalty cards is to provide rewards to regular customers to encourage continued custom, they are primarily a means of collecting huge amounts of data on individual purchasing patterns. This assists retail outlets in the layout of their stores and in targeting promotions.
- **Panels and group discussions.** Detailed questions are put to a small number of consumers. They are frequently used to discover consumers' attitudes to new products. They can also be used to collect information on changing consumer tastes and behaviour over periods of time. The **Delphi technique** involves a panel of experts assembled to provide long-term forecasts, particularly on market trends, and relies upon the panels in question reaching a consensus.
- **Test marketing.** This allows producers to try out a product on a small part of the market before a full-scale launch. Typically, television regions are used to test new products if this form of advertising is to be employed. The Wispa chocolate bar, for example, was tested in the Tyne Tees television region prior to a national launch. Test marketing allows firms to iron out major faults in products before incurring the expense of a full launch. On the other hand, it gives competitors a preview of the new product and may permit an effective counter-strategy.

1.4 Desk research

This involves using **secondary data**. A wide range of potential sources of such data are available to firms:

- **The firm's own information.** This includes existing sales data, reports from the sales team, and statistical analysis of patterns of existing sales.
- **Official data.** The government and other agencies, such as the Department of Trade and Industry and the Central Statistical Office, produce vast amounts of detailed information. Key publications include the *Annual Abstract of Statistics* and business monitors.

- **Trade associations and trade journals** supply valuable and quite specific information on market trends.
- **Mintel** and *The Economist* produce reports on the markets for all types of products.

1.5 Sampling

It is most unlikely that a firm can collect information from all the consumers to whom it is hoping to sell. Such an approach would be too expensive and time consuming. Firms need to select a sample that is **representative of the whole target market** (known as the **population**). The general principle is that the larger the sample is, the more accurate the results are likely to be.

There are a number of ways in which samples can be collected:

- **Random sampling** means that each member of the population has an equal chance of being included. This is appropriate when a firm is researching a product aimed at a large target group. Because of the difficulties inherent in selecting a genuinely random sample, computers are often used to choose people.
- **Stratified random sampling** separates the population into segments or strata. This approach can avoid bias by ensuring that the composition of the sample accurately reflects that of the entire population.
- **Quota sampling** splits the population into a number of groups, each sharing common characteristics. For example, a survey might be conducted on the views of women regarding a new product, and the number of interviewees in each age category could be clearly set out. This saves money by limiting the number of respondents, although the quotas chosen may not accurately reflect the population who may purchase the product being researched.
- **Cluster sampling** involves selecting respondents from a small area chosen to reflect the market as a whole. The producer of a new alcoholic drink, for example, may conduct intense research in one or two geographical locations.
- **Convenience sampling** is frequently used by people establishing a new business who have limited funds available. It entails sampling those consumers whom it can contact easily. Such research is susceptible to bias.
- **Snowball sampling** is a highly specialised form of sampling. It is used, for example, by firms manufacturing armaments, when businesses are unsure of their market, and entails researching one potential customer and using this contact to discover the names of other likely purchasers. The firms can then move on to research these groups before asking for further contact names.

In contrast, a business developing a consumer product, such as a new type of shampoo, will be more likely to use questionnaires and surveys among large numbers of people, most of whom will be potential customers.

1.6 Confidence levels

A confidence level measures the degree of certainty of a prediction based on a sample. For example, if the result of market research suggests that sales of a new chocolate bar will be 500,000 units per year, can the management team be confident in this result? They could only be absolutely sure if every possible purchaser was asked for an opinion. Clearly this will not happen. It is normal for a sample size to be sufficiently large to allow a 95% confidence level — that is the prediction will be proved to be correct 19 times out of 20.

1.7 An assessment of market research

Market research involves a fundamental trade-off between cost and accuracy. Firms require accurate information on which to base marketing decisions such as:
- pricing policies
- product design
- types of promotion
- market segments at which to aim the product

The greater the amount of information collected, the more reliable it should be, but the greater the cost to the firm. Clearly, if a firm has developed a multi-million pound product, then it makes sense to invest a little more to ensure that the product meets the needs of consumers as far as possible. Each set of circumstances requires a different decision. However, in each case, a business will compare expected costs and benefits.

Firms face a further dilemma. Even extensive (and expensive) market research cannot guarantee unbiased data. Respondents do not always tell the truth, samples do not always accurately reflect the entire population and the analysis of the raw data is not always correct.

2 Segmenting the market

2.1 Purposes of market segmentation

Market segmentation involves dividing a market into identifiable sub-markets, each with its own customer characteristics. Market segments may be based on differences in:
- demographics — age, sex or social class
- psychographics — attitudes and tastes of consumers
- geography — for example, the various regions of the UK

Firms engage in market segmentation in order to:
- allow different marketing techniques/media to be employed
- increase profit from each market segment
- assist in identifying new marketing opportunities
- use specialists in each of the market segments
- dominate certain segments
- reflect differences in customer tastes
- direct the marketing budget into those segments most likely to provide a higher return on the investment

2.2 Types of market segmentation

The following **seven variables** are known as **demographic factors** and form the basis of some major types of market segmentation:

- **Age.** Some goods are aimed at young people, some at old: for example, music and fashion tend to be targeted at young consumers. Firms seek to target products at the appropriate groups. High-street banks try to attract students as customers in the hope that these students will stay with them for life and because they expect students to earn relatively high salaries in the future.

- **Sex.** Some products are specifically aimed at females, others at males. Businesses do not want to waste money trying to sell products to uninterested groupings. Magazines such as *Loaded* are promoted to reach young male audiences — during televised football matches, for example.

- **Family size and life cycle.** Family size is a simple categorisation of the number of family members. Family size determines the size of pack purchased and the type of product required.

- **Psychographic or lifestyle segmentation.** This seeks to classify people according to their values, opinions, personality characteristics and interests. It concentrates on the person rather than the product, and seeks to discover the unique lifestyles of consumers. Marketers aim to discover the number of people who might fall into each of these lifestyle categories and then adapt products and services to suit the appropriate group. For example, mobile telephone companies switched from selling phones to business people to selling to other groups, such as women travelling alone.

- **Social class.** In reality, this type embraces social class and income. It is a method of segmentation which is crudely based on the occupation of the 'head of household'. It ignores second or subsequent wage earners. An example is the socioeconomic scale (Table 1.1), used by the UK market research industry to provide standardised social groupings. Similar classifications, such as the Hall Jones scale, are used elsewhere.

Social grade	Description of occupation	Example	% of population
A	Higher managerial and professional	Company director	3.0
B	Lower managerial and supervisory	Middle manager	20.4
C1	Non-manual	Bank clerk	27.2
C2	Skilled manual	Electrician	21.8
D	Semi-skilled and unskilled manual	Labourer	17.4
E	Those receiving no income from employment	Unemployed	10.2

Table 1.1 A socioeconomic scale

- **Neighbourhood classification.** This is a relatively new method of segmentation. ACORN (A Classification Of Residential Neighbourhoods) identifies 38 different types of residential neighbourhood according to demographic, housing and socioeconomic characteristics. The classification breaks the whole country down into units of 150 dwellings, with the predominant type being the classification adopted for that unit. Major users of the system include direct mail companies, financial institutions, gas and electricity companies, charities, political parties and credit card companies. ACORN was developed by CACI information services and has been widely used in siting stores and posters.

- **Education.** This is a less useful factor on which to base segmentation because it is based on the assumption that there is a strong correlation between educational

attainment, income levels and expenditure patterns. Firms target luxury products at those whom they determine to be higher income earners. Newspaper readership is often used as a proxy for education, the assumption being that more highly educated people read the broadsheets.

Two other, more specialised, variables also exist:

- **Benefit segmentation.** This groups people on the basis of why they have bought a product. Different people buy the same product for a variety of reasons. People might buy a satellite dish, for example, to watch sport, because of a special offer, to be the first in the street to have satellite or because they are bored with terrestrial television. This approach may identify an unsatisfied market segment that the business can target.
- **Usage segmentation.** This recognises that consumption rates of goods and services are not evenly distributed within the population. If a company can identify the heaviest users, it can target them in its marketing. If, for example, the firm wanted to advertise beer on television, it would be likely to choose slots in programmes that would be viewed by men.

D The marketing mix

The marketing mix refers to the main variables comprising a firm's marketing strategy. The four main elements of the mix are:

- **product** — including design, features and pack sizes
- **price** — pricing methods and tactics
- **promotion** — public relations (PR) and advertising
- **place** — distribution channels and retail outlets

These elements are sometimes referred to as the **four Ps**. Some writers identify more than four Ps, including factors such as **packaging** and **people**.

1 The product

1.1 Developing new products

The starting-point for a new product policy is a business's mission statement, which sets out its vision of the future. A business may begin its life as a single product company, but as it grows it is likely to develop other products.

> **Examiner's tip**
> Do not consider marketing issues in isolation. For example, remember that a decision on new product development will depend upon financial and human resource factors as well as the business's mission statement.
>
> A firm's product policy can develop through its **product line** or **product mix**.

1.1a Product line

If a business aims to stay with its existing market, but aims for an increased market share through extending its range of similar products, it is likely that the company will extend its product line.

Lever Brothers (part of Unilever) is noted for having a well-developed product line of detergents, including brands such as Persil, Domestos, Comfort, Lux and Surf.

1.1b Product mix

A company may decide to develop new products in order to have more than a single product line. Lever Brothers has also extended its product mix by producing Persil dishwasher liquid and Persil washing-up liquid. A benefit of this product mix is that all the products are similar and can benefit from the Persil brand name. They are all cleaning products aimed at similar market segments, so their common marketing requirements generate economies of scale.

1.2 The phases of product development

The process of developing a product varies according to the firm. However, there are six general stages:

(1) Screening ideas. Good ideas when developed will help to meet the organisation's objectives for sales volume and return on investment. Firms may use techniques such as brainstorming or scientific research to generate ideas.

(2) Concept testing. The next stage is to turn the ideas that survive the screening into tangible products that consumers will perceive as being valuable. By using market research, the company can get feedback to determine whether a need actually exists.

(3) Business analysis. Businesses develop new products or services to improve their performance. This stage sets out to estimate the potential sales, income, profit and return on investment from the new ideas.

(4) Product development. From this stage the costs incurred by the business escalate rapidly. The research and development team will now turn the idea into a product. They are concerned with design, materials, production processes, quality and safety, as well as consumers' views of the prototype product.

(5) Test marketing. Rather than launch a product nationally and risk failure, many firms prefer to conduct a test launch in a relatively small geographical area of the market. The area of the test market should be representative of the whole market and television regions are frequently chosen. However, this is not always the case. When McDonald's introduced fried chicken products, it test-marketed in a number of selected restaurants.

(6) Product launch. Launching a product is very costly. It involves many departments within the business and requires a great deal of coordination. It will be some time before the product generates enough income to repay its research and development and marketing costs.

Even when a product has passed through all these stages, success is not guaranteed. More than half of all new products fail to become established on the market.

1.3 Brands

A brand is a name given by a business to one or more of its products. Branding also establishes an identity for a product that distinguishes it from the competition. Successful branding allows higher prices to be charged and can extend its life cycle.

A **brand leader** is the product with the highest percentage sales in a market. This is important as retailers are interested in stocking popular products. This principle can make it difficult for new products to break into an established market.

Brand loyalty occurs when consumers regularly purchase particular products. Demand from such customers is unlikely to be price elastic, enabling the firm to increase the price level without much effect upon demand. Brand loyalty can be active or passive. **Active loyalty** is a preference on the part of customers for a particular product. **Passive loyalty** is the result of consumer inertia — people get used to a purchasing pattern, which they do not change. Firms introducing new products can find this a major barrier to gaining a foothold in the market.

A strong brand name is an important part of a firm's marketing strategy. It should be easy to remember and project the correct image. Popular brands are often supported by advertising slogans such as 'because you're worth it' (L'Oréal).

A firm can use two main types of branding:

- **Multiple or individual branding.** Businesses use a range of brand names for a variety of products. For example, Procter & Gamble relies on this branding policy for its line of washing products: Tide, Bold, Daz and Dreft. Multiple brands allow the firm to develop brands for particular market segments.
- **Overall family branding.** All the firm's products are branded with the same name. Virgin, Kraft, Heinz, Microsoft and Ford employ this approach. This type of branding means that the promotion of one item will promote other products within the family of products. This can increase consumer confidence in the entire range of products, so increasing sales and profits.

Firms use branding to:

- differentiate products from those of rivals
- create brand loyalty
- make demand for the product less sensitive to price changes, i.e. price inelastic
- make the product more familiar to consumers, encouraging purchasing decisions at the point of sale

2 Price

Price can be a very important marketing decision and an important determinant of the success of a product or business. For many products, price is determined in a free market by the interaction of supply and demand.

The conditions of demand are factors, other than price, which influence the level of demand for any good or service. Some of the conditions of demand are:

- **Personal tastes.** People's tastes determine their choices of goods and services and this constitutes demand. However, tastes are not permanently fixed and can be affected by the marketing activities of a business.
- **Real incomes.** As incomes rise, people purchase different items. (Real income refers to income adjusted for the rate of inflation.) Demand for luxury products (such as foreign holidays) is likely to increase at such times.
- **Other prices.** The demand for a product can depend upon the price of related goods. If the price of petrol rises, for example, the demand for cars may fall.
- **Government policies.** In nations such as the UK, the government is a major purchaser of goods and services. A change in government policy can lead to a significant change in demand for products from the construction industry, for example.

A number of factors relating to production or supply may affect the price at which products are sold:

- **Factor prices.** Changes in the price of factors of production (e.g. wages, the cost of raw materials) are likely to have an impact on the final price of the product. The extent to which the market price may be affected depends upon the relative importance of the factor of production whose price changes.
- **Techniques of production.** New inventions and techniques tend to lower costs and may reduce the market price.
- **Natural influences.** Some industries, such as construction and agriculture, are dependent upon suitable weather. Good conditions increase supply and bad conditions reduce it. In both cases, the supply curve shifts. The death of many bees in the early 1990s resulted in significant increases in the price of honey. Good harvests have led to oversupply of tea onto the world market, leading to falling prices in 2002.

2.1 Factors influencing pricing

2.1a The nature of the market

In many markets, firms have sufficient power to influence the price level at which their products are sold. A general rule is that in markets with many small firms, an individual business is likely to have little influence over the price of its products. Businesses such as hairdressers will fall into this category and are called **price-takers**. This is less likely to be the case in industries composed of a few large producers. Large-scale producers such as Cadbury's and Vodaphone can to some extent determine the price at which they sell. They are called **price-setters**. Some industries have a **price leader** — a firm which establishes prices that other businesses tend to follow rather than risk a price war.

2.1b The results of market research

Businesses can investigate the possible reactions of consumers to changes in prices through questionnaires and the use of consumer panels, as well as other forms of research. Sales staff can also conduct less formal research and report back their findings.

2.1c Other companies' products and prices

Companies will monitor competitors' products and prices, observing the effects of others' price changes and assessing likely reactions to any price changes they might implement.

2.1d Establishing patterns

Businesses might research their past records to establish patterns in the market's reaction to price changes.

2.2 Pricing methods

2.2a Cost-plus pricing

Firms first calculate the cost of producing a typical product (termed the **average cost** and calculated by **dividing the total cost of production by the number of units produced**). A 'mark-up' is then added to provide profit and to determine the final selling price. The mark-up can vary from about 30 % of average cost for groceries to 2,000 % or more for jewellery. This method ensures that some profit is made, but pays scant attention to what consumers might pay, or the prices of competitors. (See Chapter 2 for more on types of cost.)

Example

A chair manufacturer has fixed overheads of £100,000. The variable cost of each chair is £20. The business currently sells 10,000 units each year. Total costs are therefore £100,000 + £200,000 = £300,000. The average cost of each chair = £300,000/10,000 = £30.

The company opts to add 100% mark-up to the price of its chairs. The selling price will therefore be £30 plus a £30 mark-up = £60.

2.2b Contribution pricing

Also referred to as **marginal pricing**, this pricing method involves **calculating the variable cost and then adding a sum to it to represent a contribution towards fixed overheads**, as shown in Figure 1.6. Once sufficient sales have been achieved to generate enough contribution to pay the fixed overheads, any further sales will provide profit.

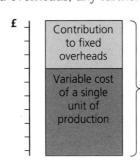

Figure 1.6 Contribution pricing

2.2c Market-based pricing

This method involves setting prices in relation to those charged by competitors. Products with little brand loyalty or reputation are often priced using this policy. Companies adopting this method may fear a price war and the uncertain effects of a prolonged period of low prices.

2.2d Price discrimination

Most markets can be divided into different segments. It is sometimes possible to separate these segments and to charge different prices. For example, providers of telephone services charge more for calls at certain times of the day. Their charges are based on the likelihood that daytime calls will be made by businesses that have to use the service during the day. Therefore, call charges are higher at these times. Evening and weekend calls are cheaper to encourage private individuals to use the service.

2.3 Pricing strategies

Pricing strategies are the medium- to long-term pricing plans that a business adopts. There are three principal pricing strategies:
- price skimming
- price leadership
- price penetration

2.3a Price skimming

Price skimming is often used when a new and innovative product is launched on to the market. It is unlikely that this product will face direct competition, at least in the short term. By setting a high price, the business will achieve a limited volume of sales but with a high profit margin on each sale. This will enable the firm to recoup some of the development costs of the product — with innovative products these might be high. The price is lowered when competitors enter the market.

2.3b Price leadership

Price leadership is used for established products with strong brand images. The firm adopting this strategy will probably dominate the market. Other firms are likely to follow this approach. It is normal for price leaders to set their prices above the current market rate.

2.3c Penetration pricing

Firms entering a market with products similar to those already available use penetration pricing. The price is deliberately set low to gain a foothold in the market and a steady gain in market share. The expectation is that, once the product is established, the price will be increased to boost profits. Companies adopting this strategy rely upon high sales to earn a reasonable level of profits.

2.4 Pricing tactics

Once a business has determined its medium- to long-term pricing strategy, there are a number of short-term pricing tactics it may employ. These include:

- **Loss leaders.** This entails setting prices very low (often below the cost of production) to attract customers. Businesses using this tactic hope that customers will purchase other (full-price) products while purchasing the loss leader. Supermarkets use this tactic extensively.
- **Special-offer pricing.** This approach involves reduced prices for a limited period of time or offers such as 'three for the price of two'.
- **Psychological pricing.** Many businesses set prices at £9.99 and £19.99 rather than £10 and £20 respectively. However, major retailers such as Marks & Spencer are using this tactic less frequently.

2.5 Price elasticity of demand

Price elasticity of demand measures the extent to which the level of demand for a product is sensitive to price changes. An increase in price is almost certain to reduce demand, while a price reduction can be expected to increase the level of demand. These general principles are straightforward, but the extent to which demand changes following a given price change is less predictable.

- **Demand is said to be price elastic if it is sensitive to price changes.** So, an increase in price will result in a significant lowering of demand and a fall in the firm's revenue. Products with a lot of competition (e.g. a brand of lager) are price elastic, as an increase in price will result in consumers switching to rival products.
- **Price-inelastic demand exists when price changes have relatively little effect upon the level of demand.** Examples of products with price-inelastic demand include petrol, basic foodstuffs and other essentials. Products with few or no substitutes often have inelastic demand.

Firms calculate their sales revenue by multiplying the sales volume by the price at which they sell their products. Elasticity plays an important part in this calculation. For example, a firm facing price-inelastic demand would enjoy higher sales revenue if it raised its price. This is because the increase in price would have relatively little impact on the volume of sales. However, this would not be a wise approach in the case of price-elastic demand. In these circumstances, a price cut would be likely to lead to increased revenue, always assuming competitors did not cut their prices too (see Table 1.2).

	Price rise	Price cut
Elastic demand	Total revenue falls	Total revenue rises
Inelastic demand	Total revenue rises	Total revenue falls

Table 1.2 Price, elasticity and total revenue

Firms would prefer to sell products with demand that is price inelastic, as this gives greater freedom in selecting a pricing strategy and more opportunity to raise prices, total revenue and profits. Firms adopt a number of techniques to make demand for their products more price inelastic:

- **Differentiating** products from those of competitors. Making a product significantly different from those available elsewhere on the market increases brand loyalty. Consumers are more likely to continue to purchase a product in the event of its price rising if they can see that it has unique features and characteristics. Advertising is frequently used to differentiate products in the minds of consumers.
- **Reducing competition** in the market through takeovers and mergers. The takeover of the German mobile phone service company, Mannesmann, by Vodaphone is a high-profile example of this trend. In recent years, many markets have seen fewer, but larger firms competing with each other. Eventually, this process results in fewer products being available to the consumer. This means that demand will be less responsive to price, and firms will be able to take advantage of this.
- **Price fixing**, which is alleged to take place in a number of markets. Through the operation of a cartel, firms can agree 'standard' prices that reduce consumer choice and influence. This technique reduces the price elasticity of the products in question.

3 Promotion

Promotion draws consumers' attention to a product or business. It aims to achieve at least some of the objectives listed below:

- attract new customers and retain existing ones
- improve the position of the business in the market
- ensure the survival and growth of the business
- increase awareness of a product
- enlarge the total market
- reach a dispersed target audience
- repair any damage done to a product or company by adverse publicity
- remind consumers about a product
- show a product is better than that of a competitor
- improve the image of a product or company
- support an existing product

Examiner's tip
It is easy to think that promotion just means advertising. Figure 1.7 emphasises that this is not the case. Analytical writing demands awareness of the circumstances in which each of the forms of promotion might be most appropriate.

As shown in Figure 1.7, promotion can be divided into two categories:

- **Above-the-line promotion**. This entails the advertising of a product or service through consumer media such as television or newspapers. Such media allow a large audience to be targeted. Most of the advertising in the UK is above the line.
- **Below-the-line promotion**. This type of promotion refers to activities such as sponsorship, trade promotions, merchandising, packaging and public relations. Below-the-line promotion uses methods over which the firm has some control.

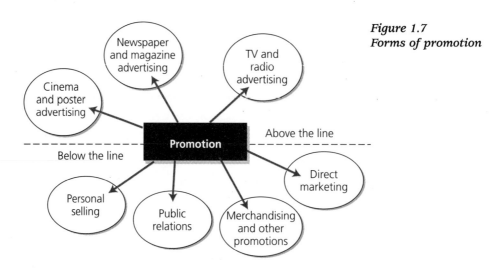

Figure 1.7
Forms of promotion

3.1 The forms of promotion

3.1a Advertising

Advertising is a paid form of non-personal communication using mass media such as television and newspapers. It aims to change the attitudes and buying behaviour of consumers. Expenditure on advertising has grown enormously over recent years, as shown in Table 1.3.

Year	Expenditure (£ billion)
1948	0.5
1980	2.2
1992	7.9
1996	10.5
2000	17.0

Source: The Advertising Association (www.adassoc.org).

Table 1.3
UK advertising expenditure, selected years

Advertising can be separated into two types:

- **Informative advertising.** This is designed to increase consumer awareness of a product. This type of advertising provides consumers with factual information. Such adverts centre upon the prices and features of the products being advertised. Examples include classified adverts in newspapers.
- **Persuasive advertising.** This attempts to get consumers to purchase a particular product. Such advertising highlights that the product in question is better than the competition. Some analysts contend that persuasive advertising distorts consumer spending by creating patterns of expenditure that may not occur naturally.

Advertising can have a number of objectives:

- **To establish demand** for a product newly launched on to the market. The profile of the product needs to be raised with targeted groups of consumers. Expenditure on this type of advertising occurs early in the life cycle and can be expensive.
- **To create strong brand loyalty.** This will occur later in the product life cycle and will emphasise the unique selling point(s) of the product. The brand name and image will be strongly promoted during the advertising campaign.
- **To defend or increase market share.** A firm faced by a competitor with a new product may implement an advertising campaign to defend its market share. At the same time, the competitor will try to use advertising to increase its market share.

- **To enter new markets.** When the Virgin Group began to sell financial services it had to spend large sums on advertising to raise public awareness of its involvement in this new market.

Businesses have a wide range of media from which to choose when planning and implementing advertising campaigns (see Table 1.4). When choosing the media for a particular campaign, a business will take into account one or more of the following:

- the cost of advertising in the various media
- the groups that the media are likely to reach
- the image portrayed by advertising in particular types of medium
- the media chosen by competitors

	Display advertising (£ million)	Classified advertising (£ million)
Television	4,646	–
National newspapers	1,711	546
Regional newspapers	919	1,844
Consumer magazines	591	158
Business and professional journals	758	512
Directories (including Yellow Pages)	–	868
Press production costs	702	–
Outdoor and transport	823	–
Radio	595	–
Cinema	128	–
Direct mail	2,049	–
Internet	155	–

Table 1.4 UK expenditure on advertising: display and classified, 2000

Advertising in the UK is subject to a number of forms of control including:

- Legal controls exercised through acts such as the Trades Descriptions Act, which prohibits untruthful advertising.
- Voluntary codes of practice operated by organisations such as the Advertising Standards Authority and the Independent Television Commission. These bodies operate industry-wide agreements concerning advertising.

3.1b Direct marketing

Direct marketing occurs when suppliers make direct contact with consumers. Examples include door-to-door selling and catalogues. One type of direct marketing is direct selling, where customers are approached directly, often by telephone. Telesales is a growing area of activity in the UK.

An aspect of direct selling that looks set to have an important future is selling via the internet. Major retailers such as Tesco operate websites through which customers can order groceries and other products for home delivery. Some internet retailers, such as the Amazon bookshop, have experienced rapid rates of growth.

Direct marketing offers businesses certain **advantages**:

- It gives them access to new segments of the market.
- It overcomes some of the disadvantages of poor retail locations.
- It may have particular relevance in a society with an ageing population.

- Markets that are **widely dispersed or difficult to reach** will usually require the services of wholesalers. Wholesalers have the facilities and expertise to deal effectively and efficiently with this type of market.
- **The technical complexity of the product.** Technically complex products are better distributed when the customer and the producer can easily contact each other to solve any problems that may arise concerning installation and operation. Computers are an example of such a product.
- **Producers selling large amounts of relatively low-priced products** are more likely to use a wholesaler. It is expensive for producers to store this type of product and they will seek the opportunity to pass on these costs to others.

Examiner's tip

Do not ignore place or distribution. It is sometimes called 'the forgotten P' and often students respond poorly to questions that are set on it. You should know the different distribution methods and which methods are appropriate in different circumstances.

Ideas for application

The emphasis that a business places on the four elements of the marketing mix will depend upon the product and the business. Firms selling luxury products, such as the Hilton Hotel in London, will emphasise the quality of their product and its place (the location in the case of the Hilton). Businesses selling necessities, such as family soap, are more likely to rely upon price and to promote their product's price competitiveness.

5 Marketing and the law

The state intervenes in the marketing activities of businesses in a number of ways:

- **Fair trading.** European Union and UK laws prohibit monopolies if they exploit their market power by, for example, charging excessive prices. Similarly, legislation prevents firms merging to form a new business that may be against the interests of consumers. Chapter 5 considers fair trading in more detail.
- **A number of acts exist to protect the consumer from marketing that is unfair.** For example, the Trades Descriptions Act (1968) makes it illegal for businesses to use false or misleading descriptions of a product's price, contents or powers. The Food Safety Act (1990) updated consumer protection in relation to food products. One clause of this act requires businesses to sell food that meets the 'substance or quality' demanded by consumers.
- **Contracts can play a large part in marketing.** For example, a contract of sale may contain a description of the product, quantities, quality, price(s) and delivery dates. If a business breaches such contracts or provides goods that are not fit for the purpose for which they are intended, it may be sued.
- **Tobacco advertising.** In February 2003 the UK government made it illegal for tobacco companies to advertise their products. The government argued that this was necessary to protect young members of society from smoking with all its consequent risks to health. The Tobacco Advertising and Promotion Act outlaws adverts in newspapers and magazines and on billboards. The Act also banned direct marketing of tobacco products from May 2003.

A2 Marketing

This section builds upon the material covered at AS. It is recommended that you re-read the AS materials alongside those that follow. Although A2 questions will focus on the following topics, it is likely that some of the principles covered at AS will be needed to support your answers.

A Taking marketing decisions

Businesses take major marketing decisions regularly. Such decisions are essential and must be successful if a business is to achieve its marketing objectives. Businesses can take two broad approaches to decision making.

1 Decisions based on hunches or instinct

It is possible for managers to take major marketing decisions, such as whether to introduce a new product, based entirely upon instinct. This means that the management team concerned conducts little or no research and relies upon its knowledge of the market.

This might be a valid approach to decision making in a market that regularly experiences rapid change, where market research cannot be used effectively. Dependence upon guesswork is, of course, a risky strategy because it is entirely possible to be wrong. Wrongly predicting a surge in demand for a product can result in a business having an embarrassing surplus of products.

2 Scientific marketing decisions

Many factors influence the markets in which businesses trade. Actions of competitors, consumers, suppliers and governments can all have an impact, as can changes in tastes and fashions. It is important to gather as much evidence as possible and to consider it carefully before taking major marketing decisions.

The marketing model outlined at the start of the AS section on marketing (page 8) can provide a framework for a scientific approach to decision making. This approach, in which gathering and analysing market research data plays a central role, does not remove the risk from these types of decision. However, it can help to reduce the risk.

B Analysing the market

1 Market- and product-orientated firms

Market orientation is the extent to which a business's strategic marketing results from considering consumers' needs and the actions of competitors. Market-orientated firms continually analyse consumers' needs and ensure that they fulfil them. Sony is an example of such a firm: the Walkman and more recently the Diskman were the result of extensive market research. A market-orientated firm will:

- predict market changes
- launch new products confidently as the chance of failure is reduced
- be prepared for changes in demand and respond promptly

Product orientation, on the other hand, is said to exist where a firm looks internally to its own production needs. Such businesses develop a technically sound product and then concentrate on selling it. This is a risky approach, as consumers may not wish to purchase the product. This philosophy is becoming less common, but classic examples remain, such as **Clive Sinclair's C5**.

2 Using statistics in marketing

We saw in the AS section that firms collect enormous amounts of data as part of the process of market research. These data are of little use without **analysis and presentation**.

2.1 Analysing data

The analysis of data enables firms to:

- forecast future sales, allowing them to produce sufficient quantities of a product to avoid the accumulation of surplus stocks or unfulfilled orders
- assess consumer reactions to the products they are selling
- estimate the future need for resources such as labour, allowing recruitment or redeployment in advance of changes in demand

Firms may need to reorganise data into a form that can be used by decision-makers in the business. It may, for example, be necessary to identify the most common figure from a range of data. This single figure can be used to represent the entire group of data. Such techniques are referred to as **measures of central tendency**. There are three principal measures of the central tendency of data:

- **The arithmetic mean** — commonly referred to as **the average**. This is calculated by adding the value of all items in the data and then dividing this total by the number of items.
- **The median** — the middle number of a range of data when the figures are placed in ascending or descending order.
- **The mode** — the most common number among a set of data. In other words, the mode is the value that occurs most frequently.

Examiner's tip

Do not concentrate solely on how to calculate the measures of central tendency. It is important to understand why businesses might want to identify a simple, representative figure.

Example

Norris Components reported the following sales figures during the first 6 months of last year:

Jan	Feb	March	April	May	June
£5,750	£6,250	£6,550	£5,975	£4,300	£6,080

Using the three measures of central tendency, we arrive at the following outcomes: The total value of the sales over the 6-month period was £34,905. When this is divided by 6 (the number of months) the **arithmetic mean** is £5,817.50.

The **median** requires the numbers to be listed in ascending (or descending) order and the central value to be chosen. In ascending order the numbers are: 4,300, 5,750, 5,975, 6,080, 6,250, 6,550. As there are an even number of figures, there is no single, central value. Hence the average is taken of the middle two: 5,975 + 6,080 = 12,055/2 = 6,027.50.

There is no **mode** in this set of data, since each figure occurs just once. This is not uncommon among sales data.

Just as firms may require a single figure to represent a range of data, so they might wish to measure the extent of dispersion of data.

The **standard deviation** is a measure of the amount of **scatter** (or **dispersion**) in a group of data. It is often represented by the Greek letter sigma (σ). It is common in many distributions for most numbers to cluster around some central value, usually the mean. However, it is also common for some values to be further away from the centre. The standard deviation measures how far away they are.

Measuring the **degree of dispersion** in data has important applications for many businesses.

- Standard deviation might be used to measure the variation from an agreed quality of a batch of products.
- It could measure the dispersion in the results of market research, giving additional information about the likely accuracy of the data.

2.2 Calculating the standard deviation

The basic formula for the standard deviation is:

$$\sigma = \sqrt{\Sigma \frac{(x - \mu)^2}{n}}$$

We can apply this formula step by step:

(1) Find the mean, μ.

(2) Find $(x - \mu)$ for each of the different individual values of x (remember, x is the individual value of the data).

(3) Find $(x - \mu)^2$ for each of the individual values of x, and then find the sum of these values $\Sigma(x - \mu)^2$.

(4) Divide $\Sigma(x - \mu)^2$ by the number of different values of x.

(5) Find the square root of $\dfrac{\Sigma(x - \mu)^2}{n}$.

Example

Norris Components produces components in batches of 100 units. A sample of 8 batches revealed the following number of defects: 2, 2, 2, 3, 3, 4, 4, 4. The standard deviation of these data is calculated as follows:

(1) x = 2, 2, 2, 3, 3, 4, 4, 4.

(2) = $\sum x/n$ = 24/8 = 3 (The arithmetic mean equals 3.)

(3) $(x - \mu)$ = –1, –1, –1, 0, 0, 1, 1, 1 (We subtract the mean from each individual value.)

(4) $(x - \mu)^2$ = 1, 1, 1, 0, 0, 1, 1, 1 (We square the results to remove the negative figures.)

(5) $\sum(x - \mu)^2$ = 6 (We add together the resulting figures.)

(6) $(x - \mu)^2/n$ = 6/8 = 0.75 (We divide the result by the number of items.)

(7) The square root of 0.75 = 0.886 (We take the square root to counter the fact that we squared the figures earlier in the calculation.)

Examiner's tip

When carrying out calculations in examinations, take care to show your workings. The majority of marks are awarded for the process, so even if you get the answer wrong, it is still possible to score quite highly. It is impossible for the examiner to award you any marks if you have not shown your calculations and you get the answer wrong.

2.3 Normal distribution

The normal distribution of data is a frequency distribution possessing a symmetrical pattern, as shown in Figure 1.9. Normal distributions tend to occur when data are collected frequently and the variations in results form the familiar pattern. **Data exhibiting a normal distribution have a number of characteristics**:

● Within a normal distribution, mode = mean = median.

● The number of results above the average will be exactly equal to the number of results below it.

● Normal distributions can be standardised so that distribution of the data has width equal to six standard deviations as shown in Figure 1.9.

The normal distribution is useful in statistical quality control. It can provide data on which components and other items subject to variation can be assessed – and rejected if necessary.

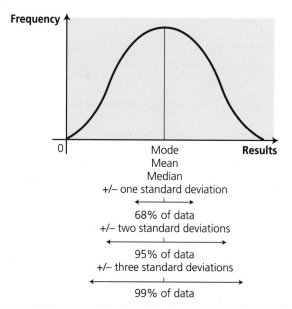

Figure 1.9
A normal distribution showing standard deviations

2.4 Analysing trends: extrapolation and correlation

A trend is an underlying pattern of growth or decline within a series of data. By establishing whether sales trends, for example, are rising or declining, a firm can plan production to ensure it can meet the demands of the market as fully as possible.

Managers are very interested in future trends in the markets in which they trade. Having an insight into future trends can assist firms in taking correct marketing decisions. Extrapolation is a relatively simple technique that can assist forecasting.

2.4a Extrapolation

Extrapolation analyses the past performance of a variable such as sales and extends this into the future. If a firm has enjoyed a steady increase in sales over a number of years, the process of extrapolation is likely to forecast a continued steady rise.

Extrapolation can assist managers in identifying market segments that are likely to experience growth or decline, so they can plan production accordingly. Extrapolation simply extends the apparent trend by eye, as shown in Figure 1.10.

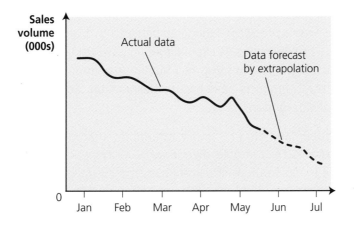

Figure 1.10
The process of extrapolation

Extrapolation has a number of advantages. It is easy to carry out, as it merely involves extending a trend and this is often done by eye. It can be completed quickly and is simple to understand.

However, it may be inaccurate because it assumes that the future will be similar to the past. For this reason it is not suitable for use in environments subject to rapid change. Predicting that sales of a fashion good, such as clothing, will continue to rise on the basis of extrapolation may be unwise, as a change in fashion may provoke a slump in sales.

2.4b Correlation

When analysing market trends, firms will attempt to identify whether there is any correlation between different variables and the level of sales. **Correlation is a statistical technique used to establish the extent of a relationship between two variables, such as the level of sales and advertising.**

Correlation can be illustrated by plotting the two variables against each other on a graph. Figure 1.11(a) plots monthly sales figures against the level of advertising expenditure for the same month. Each month's relationship is shown by an X. It is apparent that higher levels of advertising expenditure lead to higher sales. Managers may be encouraged by this result to increase spending on advertising.

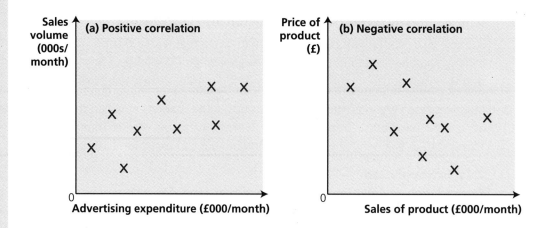

Figure 1.11 Correlation

Figure 1.11(b) shows a negative correlation between the price of a product and its sales. From this managers might decide that demand is price elastic and attempt to reduce the price as far as possible.

Correlation only shows a *possible* relationship between two variables. Sales might rise at the same time as a firm increases its expenditure on advertising. However, the two events might not be related. The rise in sales may be due to a competitor increasing prices or the fact that the firm's products have become fashionable. So the results of correlation should be treated with caution.

However, correlation can help to identify key factors that influence the level of sales achieved by a business. For example, there may be a strong positive correlation between sales and income levels. In these circumstances, the business should target markets in which consumers are enjoying rising income levels.

2.5 Analysing trends: moving averages

Moving averages are a series of calculations designed to show the underlying trend within a series of data. Moving averages can be calculated over various periods of time, although a 3-year moving average, as shown in Table 1.5, is one of the most straightforward to calculate.

Year	Bicycle sales	Three-year moving average
1993	1,500	–
1994	1,550	4,550 ÷ 3 = 1,517
1995	1,500	4,700 ÷ 3 = 1,567
1996	1,650	4,725 ÷ 3 = 1,575
1997	1,575	4,820 ÷ 3 = 1,607
1998	1,595	4,870 ÷ 3 = 1, 623
1999	1,700	5,100 ÷ 3 = 1, 700
2000	1,805	5,270 ÷ 3 = 1, 757
2001	1,765	5,470 ÷ 3 = 1, 823
2002	1,900	5,545 ÷ 3 = 1, 848
2003	1,880	

*Table 1.5
Annual sales of
George Ltd — bicycle
manufacturers*

In this example the 3-year moving average is calculated by gradually moving down the data, adding 3 years' sales together and dividing the resulting figure by 3 to obtain an average annual figure. The average figure is then plotted on the middle year of the three in question. So, for example, the moving average for 1999–2001 is plotted next to 2000.

The use of moving averages should smooth out the impact of random variations and longer-term cyclical factors including seasonal variations, thus highlighting the trend. This can assist managers in taking good quality marketing decisions as they can see the underlying pattern of sales for their products.

2.6 Presenting data

The results of data analysis can be presented as follows:

- **Pie charts** use circles to represent the categories of data. The size of the 'slice of the pie' represents the relative importance of each category of data. This is a visually effective way of presenting data, but it is not very accurate — see Figure 1.12(a).
- **Bar charts** are a common technique for presenting a range of data. The height of each individual bar represents the relative value of the data. Like pie charts, bar charts have a strong visual impact – see Figure 1.12(b).
- **Histograms** are a development of bar charts and are designed to deal with more complex forms of data. The area within the blocks is relevant here, rather than just their height.
- **Pictograms** can be visually very appealing, but they are liable to mislead unless figures are added.

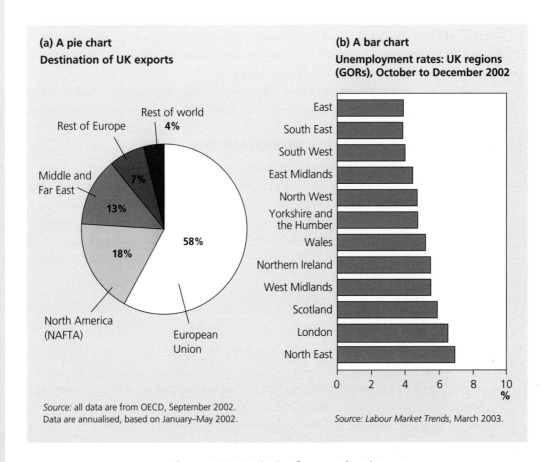

Figure 1.12 Methods of presenting data

C Marketing planning

Marketing planning is developing the tactics necessary to put into operation a marketing strategy. Marketing planning involves:
- developing a marketing plan to help the business attain its objectives
- deciding upon a marketing budget
- forecasting sales

1 *Drawing up a marketing plan*

A marketing plan is a document setting out the strategy a business will use to achieve its marketing objectives. The plan will include the following:
- Marketing targets that the firm is attempting to achieve.
- The elements of the marketing mix (place, price, promotion and product) to be used and how they will be coordinated.
- The timescale to which the plan relates (normally several years).
- The resources available to fund the marketing plan. This section will include a marketing budget (see below for more details on marketing budgets).

A marketing plan for a large organisation might bring together a number of separate marketing plans for individual goods and services.

1.1 The case for marketing planning

Businesses can gain significant benefits from drawing up marketing plans.
- Plans help to give a sense of direction to all employees within the business.
- The business's managers can compare their achievement with the plan and take the necessary action if they are not on target.
- Planning is a good process in itself. It encourages managers to think ahead and to weigh up the options open to the firm as well as to consider threats and opportunities.

1.2 The case against marketing planning

But plans have to be treated with caution too.
- Drawing up a marketing plan takes time and resources. In a rapidly changing market-place this might not be the optimal approach, as quick decisions (possibly based on hunches) might be required.
- Plans might encourage managers to be inflexible and not to respond to changes in the marketplace. Sometimes it might be more important to change the marketing targets than to achieve them.

Effective marketing plans establish marketing targets that are realistic and achievable, that motivate the staff involved and that can be afforded by the business concerned.

> *Ideas for application*
>
> Marketing planning may be more important for a business that has recently started trading, for one considering a major change, such as entering a new market, or for businesses whose marketplaces are not volatile. Thus, for example, marketing planning may have played a key role in developing the new Nissan Micra.

2 Marketing budgets

A marketing budget is the amount of money that a business allocates for expenditure on marketing activities over a particular period of time. This money is likely to be used for a variety of activities, including advertising, sales promotions, public relations and market research.

The size of a firm's marketing budget will be determined by a number of factors.

- **The financial position of the business.** If a business is recording rising profits, it is likely to be able to fund higher levels of expenditure on advertising and other marketing activities. However, it might be more sensible if a business spent more on marketing during less prosperous periods in order to increase sales and profits.
- **The actions of competitors.** If a business's rivals are increasing expenditure on marketing activities, it is likely that the firm in question will follow suit. Thus the marketing budgets of the businesses competing in the market for package holidays will rise together. Marketing, and especially advertising, is an important form of competition in many markets.
- **The business's marketing objectives.** If a firm has set objectives such as increasing market share or extending its product range, it is likely to spend heavily on marketing. Increasing market share might require substantial expenditure on advertising and sales promotions, while extending the product range may mean that the business has to invest in extensive market research.

3 Forecasting sales

Good forecasting is a key component of business success. Firms are likely to want to forecast data that relate to a number of activities:

- sales of product(s)
- costs for the forthcoming accounting period
- cash flow
- key economic variables such as inflation, unemployment, exchange rates and incomes

Time-series analysis involves forecasting future data from past figures. A firm is able to predict future sales by analysing its sales figures over previous years. Such analysis of a business's historic data can reveal patterns in those data. These patterns include the following:

- **Trends.** A trend is the underlying pattern of growth or decline in a series of data. Identifying a pattern in historic data will help the business to predict what will happen in the future. A trend can be identified by calculating and plotting the moving average using the technique explained on pages 36–37. Establishing trends helps managers to forecast sales and to ensure they have sufficient resources available so that production can meet demand.
- **Seasonality.** This relates to shorter-term fluctuations arising from the time of year. Many businesses, pubs and wine merchants, for example, enjoy higher sales at Christmas. Travel agents expect peak sales in the spring and summer, and costs of vegetables for hotels and restaurants are cheaper in the summer.
- **Cycles.** These reflect periodic changes in patterns over a period of time. It is important for a firm to establish the reasons for these cycles. The reasons may be related to fluctuations in the economy or successful (or unsuccessful) marketing activities. An example of the operation of cycles is the building industry, which suffers severely from

economic booms and recessions. In a recession, firms do not want new factories or offices, and fewer people purchase new homes.

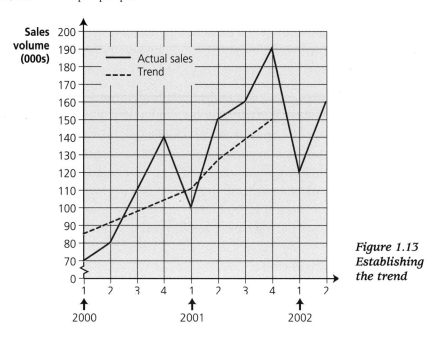

Figure 1.13
Establishing
the trend

3.1 Why do firms forecast sales?

Businesses might choose to forecast sales for a variety of reasons:
- **Sales forecasts form the basis of budgets** for many businesses. From these figures, firms can plan production levels and draw up budgets that assist in the management of the enterprise. Sales forecasts also help businesses to predict the timing of income and expenditure, and to express this information in the form of cash flow forecasts.
- Forecasts help firms **to avoid overproduction** and the possibility of selling off stock at low (and perhaps unprofitable) prices. They also help to avoid unnecessary storage costs.
- Forecasting sales provides important information about **changes in the market**. If a competitor has introduced a product, or a new business has entered the market, a firm will benefit from an accurate assessment of the impact this change may have on its sales.

3.2 Why might firms treat sales figures with caution?

Forecasting sales is a notoriously risky business. Businesses spend considerable sums of money in an attempt to make accurate forecasts, but mistakes are not uncommon. There are many reasons why the forecasts could be wrong:
- The samples on which the forecasts are based may be **too small or unrepresentative**. This could mean that the views expressed by those in the sample are not representative of the entire population of potential consumers.
- Some industries (e.g. mobile telephone or other high-technology industries) are subject to **rapid change**. Delays between gathering the data and presenting the results to those who take marketing decisions may mean that the market has changed.
- Major **changes in the external environment** can have substantial effects on the decisions of purchasers. A rise in interest rates, for example, may lead to many consumers delaying or abandoning their decision to purchase, especially if the product in question is bought on credit. Similarly, the introduction of a new competitor into the market could cause sales to plummet.

This chapter is concerned with the various areas of business finance. It looks at both the management and accounting roles within an organisation. Emphasis is placed upon the way in which financial information can be used to aid business decision making, financial monitoring and control, and to measure business performance.

AS Accounting and finance

The accounting section of the AS specifications introduces many important financial concepts, including costs, revenues and profits, cash flow and budgets. Please note that OCR and Edexcel include an introductory coverage of balance sheets and profit and loss accounts in their AS specifications. In addition, OCR covers payback and average rate of return in its AS specification. All of these topics are covered in detail in the A2 accounting and finance section, which begins on page 55.

A Introduction

1 Scope of this section

The study of accounting and finance for AS includes several topics:
- cost classification
- contribution
- break-even
- budgeting
- cost and profit centres

Each of these areas is examined in the AS section of this chapter.

2 Users and uses of financial information

2.1 Governments

Governments use the information contained in a private organisation's final accounts for the assessment of taxation, both corporation tax and VAT, and to make sure that businesses are operating legally and ethically. Governments also need to monitor the performance of public corporations, departments and other publicly owned/regulated bodies, such as the National Opera House.

2.2 Owners

Owners examine the financial information to determine whether or not their businesses are being properly managed and whether their investments are worthwhile. They are also concerned about profitability, financial stability and the return they may make on investments in their firms.

2.3 Boards of directors

Boards of directors use accounts to justify the decisions that they have made. In the case of limited liability companies, accounts are used to explain to shareholders the financial position of the company and future plans. Financial accounts can be analysed to evaluate past decisions and also to help identify possible areas of strength, weakness or inefficiency within the organisation.

2.4 Managers

The term 'managers' refers not only to those people who run an organisation, but also to those people who have a specific responsibility for an area, project or department. This covers all levels in an organisation from junior and middle managers to senior management. Junior and middle managers may analyse financial information to pinpoint aspects of inefficiency within their areas and to help them stay within their budgets or achieve targets. Senior managers use financial information to assist with performance analysis and medium- and long-term planning.

2.5 Potential investors

Comparing different organisations to try to decide which one offers the best investment opportunity is very complex. Each organisation is unique. Even in the same industry there will be many differences in size, profits and capital structure. Publicly available financial information provides investors with the basis on which a choice can be made among various investment opportunities.

2.6 Financiers

Those providing finance for private organisations will wish to assess an organisation's profitability, stability, efficiency and activity, and the comparative return on their investment. Just looking at a company's profit level is not enough. Those providing finance will want to determine the **'profit quality'** as well as judging the level of risk that an investment entails against the possible returns.

2.7 Creditors

Suppliers of goods on credit terms will examine customers' final accounts to ascertain their ability to pay, their financial stability and how long on average it actually takes them to pay suppliers. This information is essential in deciding whether or not to offer credit, how much credit to allow and what credit period a company should be given.

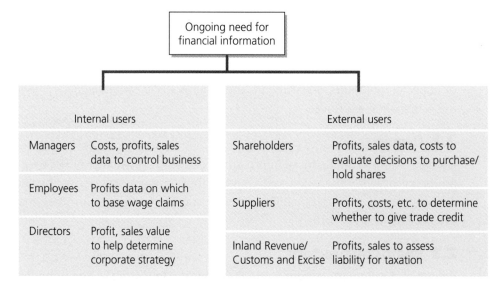

Figure 2.1 Users and uses of financial data

B Classification of costs and profit

1 *Fixed and variable costs*

1.1 Fixed costs

Fixed costs are those costs incurred by a business that **do not vary in line with changes in demand or output**, i.e. they remain constant over the time period being considered. They have to be paid whether any products are made and sold or not. Examples of fixed costs include:

- rent
- salaries
- depreciation
- interest charges

1.2 Variable costs

Variable costs are those costs incurred by a business that **vary in direct relation to the level of output and demand**, i.e. as output rises or falls, so do variable costs. Examples of variable costs include:

- materials
- components
- power
- shopfloor labour charges

2 *Direct and indirect costs*

2.1 Direct costs

Direct costs are **any costs that can be attributed as being physically embodied in the product itself**, i.e. if the product were not being made, these costs would not be incurred. By their nature, direct costs vary in direct proportion to output. Examples include:

- material costs
- labour costs

2.2 Indirect costs

Indirect costs are **any costs not attributable to products arising from business activity**. Indirect costs can be fixed or variable, but in most cases are fixed. Examples include:

- rent
- security
- depreciation
- administration

3 *Standard costs*

Standard costs are **forecasts prepared prior to production** to provide guidance on what a product should cost if production is conducted efficiently. Standard costs include:

- direct costs of labour

- direct costs of materials
- overheads relating to production as well as distribution, selling and administration

Standard costs can be used to:
- provide a basis for determining prices
- monitor and control costs through variance analysis (see pages 53–54)

4 Revenue, total costs and profit

Interrelationships between revenues, costs and profits are complex. An understanding of these relationships is important to students and managers alike.

Revenue is the total value of sales made in a time period by a business, given by:

sales revenue = quantity sold × selling price per unit

Total cost is the sum total of all costs, whatever their classification, for a given level of output over a given time period, given by:

total cost = total variable costs + fixed costs

Profit is the amount that is left over from revenue after all costs incurred in earning that revenue have been deducted, given by:

profit = sales revenue – total cost

Calculating profit may require you to use the following formula:

profit = revenue – (fixed cost + variable cost)

Example

Imagine a firm has a selling price of £10 per unit, variable cost per unit of £5 and fixed costs of £60,000.

1 Profit or loss at output and sales of 5,000 units.

		£
Sales revenue (£10 × 5,000 units)		50,000
Variable costs (£5 × 5,000 units)	25,000	
Fixed costs	60,000	
Total costs		85,000
Loss		35,000

2 Profit or loss at output and sales of 15,000 units.

		£
Sales revenue (£10 × 15,000 units)		150,000
Variable costs (£5 × 15,000 units)	75,000	
Fixed costs	60,000	
Total costs		135,000
Profit		15,000

Note how revenue *and* variable costs change when the level of output and sales is altered.

Knowing how to calculate the various component parts of a firm's costs, revenues and profit is, of course, important. However, it is the relationship between these parts that really allows analysis, planning and decision making to take place.

C Break-even analysis

Break-even occurs at the level of output at which a business's total costs exactly equal its revenue or earnings and neither a profit nor a loss is incurred.

1 The break-even point

At break-even point the business has made insufficient sales to make a profit, but sufficient sales to avoid a loss. In other words, it has earned just enough to cover its costs.

This occurs when **total cost = sales revenue**.

Break-even analysis can provide businesses with important information, but the most important element of this information is an indication of how much the firm needs to produce (and sell) in order to make a profit.

2 Determining the break-even point

The easiest way of representing the break-even point is through the use of a break-even chart or diagram as shown in Figure 2.2. The step-by-step points below explain how to draw a break-even chart.

(1) Give the chart a title.

(2) Label axes (horizontal — output in units; vertical — costs/sales in pounds).

(3) Draw on the fixed cost line.

(4) Draw on the variable cost line.

(5) Draw on the total cost line.

(6) Draw on the sales revenue line.

(7) Label the break-even point where sales revenue = total cost.

(8) Mark on the selected operating point (SOP), i.e. the actual or forecast level of the company's output.

(9) Mark on the margin of safety (the difference between the SOP and the break-even level of output).

(10) Mark clearly the areas of profit and loss.

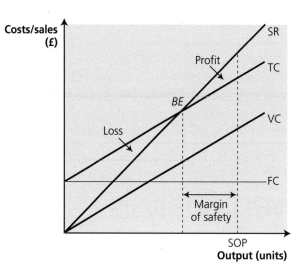

Figure 2.2
A break-even chart
for product X

3 Calculating break-even

Although representing the break-even point in diagrammatic form makes it clear and easy to understand, it is not really necessary. The break-even point can be calculated using the formula:

$$\text{break-even in units of output} = \frac{\text{fixed costs}}{\text{selling price} - \text{variable cost per unit}}$$

Example

Look again at the example of calculating profits and losses on page 44. The firm in question sold its products for £10 each, incurred a variable cost on each unit of £5 and had fixed costs of £60,000. Using the formula above:

$$\text{break-even} = \frac{60,000}{(£10 - £5)} = \frac{60,000}{5} = 12,000 \text{ units}$$

Thus if the firm produces and sells 12,000 units its costs will exactly equal its revenues and it will break even.

4 The usefulness of break-even

Break-even has several major uses as outlined below.

4.1 Starting a new business

A new business can estimate the level of sales required before it would start to make a profit. From this, it can see whether or not its business proposal is viable or not.

4.2 Measuring profit and losses

In diagrammatic form, break-even enables businesses to tell at a glance what their estimated level of profit or loss would be at any level of output and sales.

4.3 Modelling 'what if?' scenarios

Break-even enables businesses to model what would happen to their level of profit if:
- they put their selling price up

- there was an increase in variable costs
- fixed costs were to change for any reason

They can also use break-even to find out how much margin of safety they have and, consequently, what fluctuations in market demand they might survive.

5 Limitations of break-even

Break-even analysis is quick to perform but a simplification. As such, it has several short-comings:

- **No costs are truly fixed.** A stepped fixed cost line would be a better representation, as fixed costs are likely to increase in the long term and at higher levels of output if more production capacity is required.
- A linear (straight) variable cost line takes **no account of economies of scale and discounts** such as bulk buying.
- The total cost line should not, therefore, be represented by a straight line.
- Sales revenue assumes that all output produced is sold and at a uniform price, which is **unrealistic**.
- **Break-even is a static model** and needs to be reworked every time there is a minor fluctuation in any of the variables.
- **The analysis is only as good as the information provided.** Collecting accurate information is expensive, and in many cases the cost of collection would outweigh any benefit that break-even analysis could provide.

D Contribution

1 Definition

Contribution is the difference between sales revenue and variable cost. It is calculated using the following formula:

contribution = sales revenue − variable costs

Contribution is a simple concept, yet one which is very important to many businesses, particularly to those that produce a number of products.

Contribution is used in the first place to pay a company's fixed overheads, which instead of being allocated to products have been placed on one side. Once these have been covered, any additional contributions are used to provide profits for the company.

Example

A business might produce two products: A and B.

	Product A	**Product B**
Price per unit	£10	£25
Variable cost per unit	£6	£15
Sales (units)	10,000	35,000
Total contribution	£40,000	£350,000

In each case, we have simply deducted the variable cost of production from the selling price of the product before multiplying by sales to arrive at total contribution.

2 Contribution per unit

The idea of contribution works along the lines that **each individual product has to make a contribution to the overall running costs of the firm**. As long as the selling price of an individual product is greater than the variable costs associated with producing the product, the product will make a contribution to paying the overheads of the business and eventually generate profit.

Using the concept of contribution in a multi-product firm avoids the need to divide up fixed overheads among the various products. This can be arbitrary and inaccurate.

Contribution per unit can be calculated in two ways:

(1) **unit selling price − unit variable costs = contribution per unit**

(2) $\dfrac{\textbf{total sales revenue − total variable cost}}{\textbf{output}}$ **= contribution per unit**

3 Contribution and break-even

The theory of contribution tells us that if each product makes a contribution, and all these contributions are added up and used to pay fixed costs, any contributions remaining at this point are profit.

This enables us to use the theory of contribution to calculate break-even and profit for any given situation. The question is: how many individual contributions are needed to pay fixed costs? This is given by:

$$\frac{\textbf{fixed costs}}{\textbf{contribution per unit}} = \begin{array}{c}\textbf{number of}\\\textbf{contributions needed}\end{array} = \begin{array}{c}\textbf{level of output}\\\textbf{to break even}\end{array}$$

At this point, enough contributions have been made to pay fixed costs. Variable costs have already been accounted for because: contribution = sales revenue − variable cost.

This is a very useful formula, as it enables companies to model 'what if' scenarios quickly and easily without having to redraw break-even charts all the time.

E Cash-flow management

1 Cash-flow forecasting

A cash flow is used to show when money is expected to flow into and out of a business over a period of time. It also shows where the money comes from and how it is expected to be spent. There are certain times for some businesses when payments will be larger than revenue. During these periods it is important that there are sufficient funds to meet these payments. If not, the business may be unable to obtain vital supplies, pay for electricity or gas and, in severe cases, meet loan or mortgage payments. A business may need to arrange a loan (probably an overdraft) to cover such periods.

Examiner's tip
The difference between cash inflows and outflows is not profit. Profit can be affected by non-cash items such as depreciation and stock valuation. Furthermore, if a business either offers or receives goods on credit, these sales and purchases have still been made, even though no cash has changed hands. A highly profitable business can therefore experience cash-flow problems. This is especially true in manufacturing companies, where the time lag involved in purchasing, processing, selling and receiving payment for goods can be considerable.

2 Purposes of cash-flow forecasting

Cash-flow forecasting is used to:
- forecast when cash outflows might exceed cash inflows
- plan when and how to finance major items of expenditure
- ensure that liquid assets are available to meet payments
- highlight any periods when cash surpluses may exist that could be more profitably invested elsewhere
- justify to lenders that any borrowed funds can and will be repaid

3 The construction of a cash-flow forecast

Cash-flow forecasts are constructed using a combination of historical information, trend analysis and expectations on the part of the business. They comprise three sections:
- **Receipts** — recording the expected total month-by-month receipts.
- **Payments** — recording the expected monthly expenditure by item.
- **Running balance** — keeping a running balance of the expected bank balance at the beginning and end of each month (see Figure 2.3).

4 Methods of improving cash flow

- **Factoring.** This is particularly useful for small businesses that may experience difficulty in controlling credit. Factoring enables a business to sell its outstanding debtors to a specialist debt collector called a **factor**. The business will receive approximately 80% of the value of the debt immediately. The factor then receives payment of the bill

and are given only after an independent survey of the asset. In addition, a comprehensive report on the business's past and future expected performance is compiled. A mortgage loan is one that is usually secured on land or buildings for periods of 20 years or longer.

- **Debentures.** These are secured against specified or unspecified assets. Only very large and established companies issue debentures. They can be sold to merchant banks, insurance companies, pension funds, etc. Debentures can only be issued to members of the public by public limited companies (plcs).
- **Issuing shares.** An established company may be able to issue further shares to its existing shareholders at a favourable rate in order to obtain more funds. Alternatively, if the company is a plc, it can place the shares with a financial institution, which will sell them, or they can be traded directly on the stock exchange.
- **Government and European Union support.** Financial help in the form of grants or subsidies is also available from a variety of sources, such as national and local governments, and the European Union.

Ideas for application

It is important to consider the type of business when answering questions on sources of funds. It may seem obvious, but relatively few students suggest that companies can raise funds by selling shares. In addition, if the business in question has valuable assets, a sale-and-leaseback deal may be appropriate.

G Budgeting

1 Preparation of budgets

A budget is a forecast of costs or revenues. Its purpose is to provide a target for management as well as to provide a basis for a later review of performance.

A key point is that **a budget needs to be prepared for a particular purpose**. It must have a specific set of objectives or targets attached. If not, the budget is meaningless.

Budgets can be prepared for individual projects, departments or cost centres. When all the individual budgets are drawn into one budget for the whole company, the result is called the **master budget**.

Other types of budget exist, including:
- **Flexible budgets.** These are designed to adjust as businesses experience change. Such budgets can cope with changes in prices and costs as well as in the quantities sold.
- **Operating budgets.** These set out the day-to-day expenditure and revenue of the business. The main operating budget is the **profit budget**.
- **Zero-based budgets.** These require managers responsible for budgets to justify any money they require. Otherwise their budget is set at zero to avoid budgets creeping up each year in line with inflation or other measures.

2 Setting budgets

The detail and the content of the budget should be the result of negotiation with all concerned. Those responsible for keeping to a budget should play a part in setting it, if it is to work as an effective motivator.

The costs built into budgets can be based on **historic costs** (past figures) or **standard costs** (theoretical costs built up from work-studies within the business).

3 Benefits of budgets

- Targets can be set for each section, allowing management to identify the extent to which each section contributes to the overall objectives of the business.
- Attention is drawn to inefficiency and waste, so that appropriate remedial action can be taken.
- Budgets make managers think about the financial implications of their actions and focus decision making on the achievement of targets and corporate objectives.
- Budgeting should improve financial control, if only because employees are aware that their actions are being scrutinised.
- Budgets can help improve internal communication.
- Delegated or devolved budgets can be used as a motivator by giving employees authority and the opportunity to fulfil some of their higher-level needs, as identified by Maslow (see pages 80–81). At the same time, senior managers retain control over the business by monitoring budgets.

4 Drawbacks of budgets

- The operation of budgets can become inflexible. For example, sales may be lost if the marketing budget is strictly adhered to at a time when competitors are undertaking major promotional campaigns.
- Budgets have to be reasonably accurate to have any meaning. Wide differences (or variances) between budgeted and actual figures can demotivate staff and call the whole process into question.

5 Variance analysis

Variance analysis is the study by managers of the differences between planned activities/results in the form of budgets and the actual results that were achieved. Table 2.1 is an example of a labour budget for a manufacturing process.

Cost centre	Grade (£)	Budgeted (£)	Actual (£)	Variance (£)	
Lathes	Electricians	720	730	(–10)	Adverse
	Engineers	120	180	(–60)	Adverse
	Operators	400	350	+50	Favourable
Drills	Setters	1,440	1,520	(–80)	Adverse
	Operators	1,000	1,100	(–100)	Adverse

Table 2.1 A labour budget

As the period covered by the budget unfolds, actual results can be compared with the budgeted figures and variances examined.

A positive (or favourable) variance occurs when costs are lower than forecast or revenues higher.

A negative (or adverse) variance arises when costs are higher than expected or revenues are less than anticipated.

Positive variances might occur because of good budgetary control or by accident: for example, due to rising market prices. Negative variances might occur due to inadequate control or factors outside the firm's control, such as rising raw material costs.

Examiner's tip
Just because a result is favourable does not mean that everything is in order. Neither does an adverse variance mean that the area responsible has been inefficient. A favourable production material variance could be generated from using lower-quality raw materials, which in turn could manifest itself as a drop in sales. Look at the reason for the variance, not just the variance itself.

Ideas for application
As with cash flow, make sure you read the figures carefully before responding to analytical and evaluative questions about budgets and variance analysis. In addition, make sure that you look for and draw on relationships between the figures. Thus if sales revenue has risen, it would not be surprising if variable costs have too.

H Cost and profit centres

1 Cost centres

A cost centre is a specific and discrete department, area or person within a business organisation from which costs can be ascertained and to which costs can be allocated.

2 Profit centres

A profit centre is an area, department, division or branch of an organisation that is allowed to control itself separately from the larger organisation. It makes its own decisions, following corporate objectives, and produces its own profit and loss account for amalgamation with the rest of the business.

3 Advantages and disadvantages of cost/profit centres

3.1 Advantages
- Decentralised decision making allows areas to make decisions faster and be more responsive to changes in local conditions.

- Delegated power and authority to centres improves motivation.
- It is easier to generate a good teamworking spirit in smaller, more autonomous groups.
- Allocating costs and profits on a specific area basis allows for more accurate decision making.
- Monitoring of budgets, targets and performance is much easier with smaller areas.

3.2 Disadvantages

- Cost and profit centre allocation can cause rivalry between centres, with centres competing among each other rather than with other businesses.
- Individual centres can become too narrowly focused and lose sight of overall business objectives.
- Communication between centres can become difficult and slow.
- Coordinating the activities of many small areas is complex.
- Performance of individual areas may be adversely or favourably affected by local conditions, making it difficult to analyse.
- The allocation of costs can be complicated, expensive and inaccurate. Costs can act as a demotivator if managers do not take ownership of them because they feel the costs have been imposed.

A2 Accounting and finance

This section builds upon the material covered at AS. It is recommended that you re-read the AS materials alongside those that follow. Although A2 questions will focus on the following topics, it is likely that some of the principles covered at AS will be needed to support your answers.

A Introduction

1 Scope of this section

A2 accounting and finance covers a wide range of areas including:
- advanced break-even
- company accounts
- ratio analysis
- investment decision making

Each of these areas is examined in the A2 section of this chapter.

2 Definitions

Useful definitions include:

Accounting — the systematic recording of the financial information of a business over a given time period. The principal accounts compiled are profit and loss accounts, balance sheets and cash-flow statements.

Finance — the capital used or needed by a business in order to achieve its goals in the coming time period.

Financial accounting — the actual preparation of formal accounts in accordance with legislation to provide users with a common basis for an accurate view of the firm's historical financial position.

Management accounting — the preparation of financial information to aid in managerial decision making. Management accounting is used primarily for the analysis of alternative decisions, planning, review of performance and monitoring of the firm's position, rather than as a historical record of financial events.

B Using contribution and break-even

1 Contribution

Break-even and contribution are useful techniques for decision making. The concept of contribution was an important one in AS Business Studies and was used in calculating the break-even point. We saw that it can be calculated by use of the formula below:

sales – variable costs = contribution

Contribution has two potential uses. First, it is available to pay fixed costs incurred by a business. Any contribution remaining after this transaction is profit for the business:

contribution – fixed costs = profit

Contribution can also be used to calculate the level of profits for a business producing a number of products. It can provide managers with a clearer perspective of the performance of a particular business — or part of a business.

2 Contribution costing

Contribution costing does not include fixed costs in the calculation. Contribution costing is valuable in a business that has several products or factories. If a product earns enough revenue to pay its fixed costs, it may be viewed positively by the business's managers, who recognise that fixed costs have to be paid anyway. In these circumstances, the product will generate a positive contribution and assist in covering fixed costs or generating profit.

Example

Product	Star	Planet	Sun
Revenue (£000)	914	568	232
Variable costs (£000)	700	610	101
Contribution (£000)	214	(42)	131

In the example above, stars and suns generate a positive contribution that can be used to pay

fixed costs and possibly to provide profits. However, planets have variable costs that are higher than sales revenue.

The managers may decide to end production of planets, but any decision would take into account the following factors:

- Whether these figures represent a typical trading performance for the business. It might be that sales have slumped temporarily and are expected to improve.
- Whether the firm is able to sell more stars and suns as a result of ceasing production of planets. Having idle capacity may not improve the business's financial position.
- What will happen to fixed costs. If fixed costs do not fall, the firm might be better off continuing production. Otherwise the fixed costs will have to be borne by stars and suns, reducing their profitability.
- Non-financial factors. For example, industrial relations within the business might be damaged seriously by a decision to cease production of planets because of the job losses that may result.

It is possible to calculate the profitability (or otherwise) of this firm, as long as fixed costs are known. If the firm in question had fixed costs of £250,000, it would earn a profit of £55,000. This is calculated by totalling the contribution earned by stars, planets and suns (214 + 131 – 42), which is £303,000. Profit is calculated by subtracting fixed costs from total contribution. So profits are £53,000 (£303,000 – £250,000).

3 Contribution and pricing

Contribution pricing offers a number of **advantages**:

- The technique of contribution allows a company to analyse each product in terms of it being able to cover its own variable costs. Prices can be set in relation to the **'true' price** of producing that good rather than an inflated cost that includes fixed costs.
- Using contribution pricing, **businesses can enjoy more flexibility in their pricing decisions**. Successful products can be priced to make a high level of contribution, whereas less successful or maturing products can be priced to make a lower contribution. In this way, such products still help towards the company's fixed costs and enable the company to maintain a larger product range. Alternatively, a product can be priced to make differing levels of contribution throughout its product life cycle. The price of a games console when first released might be high, but it might decline later as more rival products appear.
- Contribution pricing **allows new products to be introduced and tested on the market**, as long as they can show that they can cover their own direct costs of production and make a positive contribution towards the fixed costs.
- Contribution pricing may lead to companies adopting **price discrimination**, whereby they charge different groups of consumers different prices for the same product. BT does this in relation to peak and off-peak calls and business and domestic users. Contribution pricing allows a company to operate price discrimination with greater certainty.
- A company may make a deliberate decision to price its product below variable cost. The product will therefore be sold at a loss. Firms operate **loss leaders** in order to attract customers to purchase other products on which they make a profit.

4   *Special order decisions*

An important facet of contribution pricing is the effect it has on decisions regarding additional customer orders at non-standard prices. These are sometimes termed 'special order decisions'.

Two special order situations may occur. The second is more likely to appear as part of an examination question.

- **The customer offers a price that is higher than the usual selling price.** This scenario is most likely to occur in circumstances in which the customer has special requirements. Examples include a quick delivery time or slightly different product specifications. Either case could cause problems for the company. It may be that meeting such an order results in increased costs, such as overtime payments, meaning that profits are lower than initially expected. Such orders therefore require careful deliberation.
- **The customer offers a price below the usual selling price.** The acceptability of such an order depends on the price being offered and the production capacity available to the company.

Even if fulfilling an order would make a positive contribution, the decision about whether or not a company accepts it is subject to a number of provisos:

- That it possesses spare capacity (i.e. production capacity that is currently idle).

- That it will not have to pay overtime to employees, which would result in a higher variable cost per unit of production and might mean the company making lower profits.
- That the customer it is selling to is unable to resell these products to existing customers at a lower price than that normally paid.
- That existing customers remain unaware that the products are being sold at a reduced price.

5 Absorption costing

An alternative to contribution costing used by multiproduct firms involves treating each of a firm's products as separate from the remainder of the firm's operations. **Absorption costing calculates the unit cost of an item including some fixed as well as variable costs. In this way, all fixed costs are allocated to (or absorbed by) the products made.**

A firm that produces a range of products may decide to divide up its overheads and allocate them to its product range on the basis of:
- the proportion of factory space used by the product
- the percentage of the workforce employed in producing each product range
- the share of sales revenue earned by each of the products

Apportioning fixed costs in this way has drawbacks:
- It is essentially **arbitrary**. Different companies use different methods. For example, one company might apportion fixed costs according to production line time, while another company making similar products might decide to allocate fixed costs according to the number of employees working upon each product. The two companies, both with the same product, would calculate that the products have different total costs.
- **Employees may become somewhat demotivated** if they discover that 'their' product has been allocated a share of fixed overheads that they consider unfair.

Contribution concentrates on the relationship between revenues earned and costs incurred by a particular product or area. As long as a product is making a **positive contribution**, there is a case for continuing to produce the product in the short term while considering the options available. In this way, a product manager does not need to take account of any arbitrarily allocated fixed costs.

6 Advanced break-even analysis

We saw in the AS section on accounting and finance that break-even is the level of output at which total costs are exactly equal to revenue from sales and that neither a profit nor a loss is made. Our analysis of break-even at AS presented break-even as a static model that could not represent changes in key variables such as price and costs.

However, break-even analysis can illustrate the effects of changes in price and costs and assist managers in making decisions when:
- an order is received at a price which differs from that normally charged
- the firm faces an increase or decrease in fixed or variable costs

Using break-even analysis in these circumstances, managers can decide whether it is likely to be profitable to meet an order or to continue production. This aspect of break-even analysis makes it a more valuable technique. After all, few businesses trade in environments in which changes in prices and costs do not occur regularly.

Table 2.2 illustrates the effects of changes in key variables on the break-even chart. These are further illustrated in Figures 2.4a, 2.4b and 2.4c.

Change in key variable	Impact on break-even chart	Effect on break-even output	Explanation of change	Illustrated in Figure
Increase in selling price	Revenue line pivots upwards	Break-even is reached at a lower level of output	Fewer sales will be necessary to break even because each sale generates more revenue while costs have not altered	Figure 2.4(a)
Fall in selling price	Revenue line pivots downwards	A higher level of output is necessary to reach break-even	Each sale will earn less revenue for the business and, because costs have not altered, more sales will be required to break even	Figure 2.4(a)
Rise in fixed costs	Parallel upward shift in fixed and total cost lines	Break-even occurs at a higher level of output	More sales will be required to break even because the business has to pay higher costs before even starting production	Figure 2.4(b)
Fall in fixed costs	Parallel downward shift in fixed and total cost lines	Smaller output is needed to break even	Because the business faces lower costs, fewer sales will be needed to ensure that revenue matches costs	Not illustrated, but opposite of above
Rise in variable costs	Total cost line pivots upwards	Higher output is needed to break even	Each unit of output costs more to produce, so a greater number of sales will be necessary if the firm is to break even	Not illustrated, but opposite of fall in variable costs
Fall in variable costs	Total cost line pivots downwards	Lower level of output is needed to break even	Every unit of production is produced more cheaply, so lower output and sales are necessary to break even	Figure 2.4(c)

Table 2.2 Effects of changes in key variables on the break-even chart

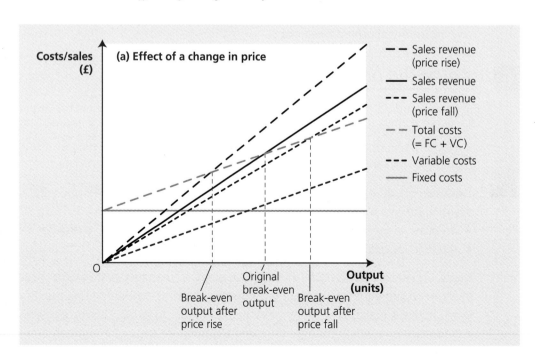

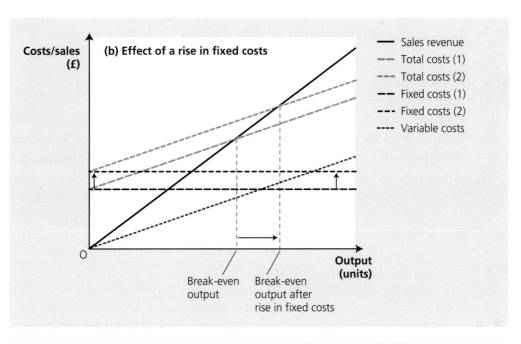

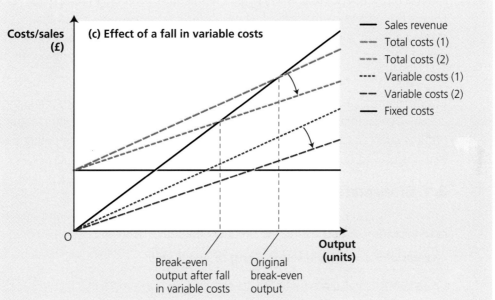

Figure 2.4 Effects of changes in key variables on the break-even chart

Note: Figure 2.4(b) only illustrates a rise in fixed costs to avoid the figure becoming too complex. A fall in fixed costs would have the exact opposite effect. Figure 2.4(c) only illustrates a fall in variable costs to avoid the diagram becoming too complex. A rise in variable costs would have the exact opposite effect.

Examiner's tip

It is unlikely that you will be asked to construct a break-even chart from scratch in an A2 examination because it would take too long. However, a question requiring you to demonstrate the effects of changes in a key variable by adding on the relevant lines is quite possible. You should be confident in doing this. Because all the lines on a break-even chart are straight, you only need to calculate the change at zero output and the maximum output, mark these points and draw a straight line joining them. Practise this, preferably using past papers.

C Company accounts

1 The role of accounting and finance in business

Accounting and finance operations within an organisation fulfil many different purposes — from legal and statutory requirements for limited companies as outlined in the Companies Acts of 1985 and 1989, to providing a wealth of information for the wide range of stakeholders interested in the financial make-up of a particular organisation. The financial records of public limited companies are available as part of their annual report and accounts. These reports provide an overview of companies' activities as well as a great deal of financial information.

2 Profit and loss accounts

A profit and loss account is an accounting statement that shows a firm's sales revenue generated over a trading period and all the relevant costs incurred in earning that revenue. **Profit** is the difference that arises when a firm's sales revenue is greater than its total costs. **Loss** is the difference that arises when a firm's sales revenue is less than its total costs. **Making a profit is one of the most significant business objectives.** It is the profit incentive, the reward to be gained, that motivates people towards starting out in business in the first place.

In simple terms, a profit and loss account measures the level of profit made by the organisation. In accounting terms, the word 'profit' on its own has very little actual meaning. Profit is such an integral objective and such a good indicator of company performance that it is broken down into two main types.

2.1 Gross profit

Gross profit is the measure of the difference between sales revenue and the cost of manufacturing or purchasing the products that have been sold.

> **gross profit = sales revenue – cost of goods sold**

Gross profit is calculated without taking into account costs that could be classified as expenses (e.g. administration, advertising) or overheads (e.g. rent, rates).

It is a useful measure. For example, if Company A and Company B are providing a similar good or service and Company A is making a lower level of gross profit than Company B, Company A must look closely at its trading position. It could try to find a cheaper supplier.

2.2 Net profit

After calculating gross profit, the next stage is to remove all other expenses and overheads (those costs which are not directly concerned with the trading activities of the business). The result is net profit.

> **net profit = gross profit – (expenses + overheads)**

Again, net profit is a very useful measure. A business may find itself making a very healthy gross profit but a very small net profit in comparison to its competitors. This may be because its overheads are not under control. Calculating both gross and net profit allows owners/managers to identify problem areas with greater ease.

3 Profit and loss account layout

All profit and loss accounts follow the same basic three-section structure:

Section 1: the trading account. This is concerned with calculating profit made on trading activities, i.e. **gross profit**.

Section 2: the profit and loss account. This is concerned with the overall level of profit made by a business, i.e. **net profit**.

Section 3: the appropriation account. This is concerned with showing how any profits made by the business have been distributed, i.e. where the profits have gone.

Example

Pearson Ltd: trading, profit and loss account for the period ended 30 May 2003

	£
Sales	2,500,000
Less Cost of goods sold	1,300,000
Gross profit	1,200,000
Add Other income	
Less Expenses:	
Administration expenses	320,000
Selling and distribution expenses	200,000
Finance expenses	130,000
Net profit for the year before taxation	550,000
Less Corporation tax	113,000
Profit for the year after tax	437,000
Add Profit and loss account balance	42,000
	479,000
Less: Transfer to general reserve	79,000
Ordinary dividend	250,000
Retained profit carried forward to next year	150,000

From the appropriation account it can be seen exactly how much profit has been shared out in dividends and how much has been kept by the company, as well as the amount of tax paid. This lets all those concerned know exactly what has happened to the business's profit.

Note: sole traders do not need an appropriation account.

3.1 Profit quality

Profit quality measures whether or not an individual profit source will continue. A company may make one-off profits from the sale of assets, but these may not be a sustainable source of profits and, if so, will be termed low-quality profit. On the other hand, a company with a strong trading position, which can be expected to make profits in future years, is described as generating high-quality profits.

Examiner's tip

This is an important concept to take into account when responding to questions that ask you to consider a company's financial position.

3.2 Profit utilisation

Companies may use profit in two main ways:

- **Retained profits.** These are the share of profits kept by the company and added to the company's balance sheet reserves. Retained profits increase the value of the company, so helping an organisation to expand.
- **Distributed profits.** These are the portion of a company's profit shared out to external parties, such as owners or partners, preference shareholders, ordinary shareholders and the Inland Revenue (in the form of corporation tax).

4 Capital and revenue expenditure

4.1 Revenue expenditure

Revenue expenditure refers to spending on all items apart from fixed assets. Examples include:

- materials
- selling and distribution costs
- wages/salaries
- administration costs
- fuel
- depreciation

Although depreciation is a charge against a capital item (fixed asset), it is included here because it is supposed to represent the amount of that item consumed during the time period in question. This type of expenditure is shown on the profit and loss account.

4.2 Capital expenditure

Capital expenditure is spending on items that can be used over and over again. This means their benefit will be spread over more than 1 year. This type of expenditure is on fixed assets and affects the balance sheet of a firm. It has no direct effect on the profit and loss account. The cost of capital expenditure is spread over the asset's useful life via depreciation. Examples include:

- land
- buildings
- machinery
- vehicles
- fixtures and fittings
- furniture

5 Balance sheets

The balance sheet is an accounting statement of the firm's assets and liabilities on the last day of an accounting period. The balance sheet lists the assets that the firm owns and sets these against the balancing liabilities — the claims of those individuals or organisations that provided the funds to acquire the assets.

Assets take the form of fixed assets and current assets, while **liabilities** take the form of capital, long-term liabilities and current liabilities. The balance sheet can be seen as a 'snapshot' of the firm's current state of affairs at a given time.

- **Fixed assets** are those assets, such as machinery, equipment and vehicles, that are bought for long-term use (generally taken to be more than a year) rather than for resale.
- **Current assets** (or circulating assets) are items such as stock, debtors, bank and cash that will be converted into cash by the end of the financial year.

A business's assets will automatically be matched by its **liabilities**.

 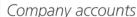

- **Capital** (also known as **owners' capital**, **equity capital** and **capital invested**) is the funds invested in a business in order to acquire the assets that the business needs to trade. It is a liability because the business technically 'owes' it to the investors.
- **Long-term liabilities** are moneys employed in the business that have been borrowed from external sources which will be repaid over the 'long term' (a period longer than 1 year). Long-term liabilities include such things as mortgages, bank loans and debentures.
- **Current liabilities** are debts of the business that will be repaid in the 'short term' (less than 1 year). The most common current liabilities are creditors and bank overdrafts.

All businesses have a variety of assets and liabilities. Table 2.3 summarises these and provides examples.

Fixed assets	Current assets	Other assets	Capital	Long-term liabilities	Current liabilities
The conventional way to list assets begins with the most illiquid first, i.e. the asset which is most difficult to turn into cash without a loss in its value, and ends with the most liquid asset.			All these are classed as liabilities, even capital, as they are all monies that at some point will need to be repaid, i.e. if the owners sell the business they will want their money back.		
Tangibles	**Stock** — goods made or bought for resale.	**Stocks and shares** — held in other companies which will provide the organisation with a financial return or dividend.	Includes money invested as well as other resources. It is more than likely, for example, that someone setting up a business will donate the car he or she already owns to the business rather than purchasing a new one. Also includes shares and reserves, e.g. share premium account.	**Loans** — money borrowed from an outside agency usually carrying a fixed repayment date and interest charge.	**Creditors** — suppliers from whom the business has purchased goods and not yet paid.
Freehold land — land over which the owner has absolute rights and doesn't have to pay rent.					
Freehold buildings — as above.	**Debtors** — clients who have purchased goods but who have not yet paid.				**Accruals** — goods and services which have been used and not yet paid for.
Leasehold land — a lease is a legal agreement between the owner of a property and another person to the effect that the other person has use of the property for an agreed period of time.	**Prepayments** — items for which the business has paid in advance of the date of the balance sheet, e.g. car insurance.	**Loans** — the situation may arise where the organisation lends another business money. This loan is an asset as the organisation making the loan is receiving the benefit of interest payments.		**Mortgage** — a form of commercial loan usually secured against a specific property asset. May or may not be a fixed rate of interest.	**Provision for repayment of debts expected to mature** — loans falling due, taxation and dividend payments.
Plant/machinery/equipment — anything from specialised machinery used in manufacture to computers or even furniture.	**Cash at bank** — monies held in a bank or other institution's accounts.			**Debenture** — an alternative to selling shares, a form of fixed repayment and interest loan stock.	
Vehicles — all types.					
Intangibles	**Cash in hand** — physical notes and coins held by the business in safes, tills or as petty cash.				
Goodwill — the prestige a business enjoys which adds value over and above the value of its physical assets.					
Patents/copyright — exclusive rights to make or sell a particular invention.					
Trademarks — build up brand loyalty and thus can be ascribed a value like goodwill.					

Table 2.3 Assets and liabilities

The assets owned by a business are financed by its liabilities. If all the assets of the business are listed on one side of the balance sheet and all the liabilities of the business are listed on the other, the two totals should balance. This is usually shown vertically, as in Figure 2.5.

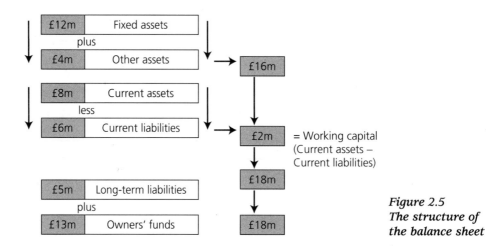

Figure 2.5
*The structure of
the balance sheet*

6 Accounting principles

A number of principles must be followed when preparing accounting records and summarising them in financial statements.

6.1 Consistency

All accounting information should be consistent between one year and the next. For example, there should not be a change in the method of depreciation used. This allows accurate comparisons to be made.

6.2 The going concern principle

This suggests that all financial records are based on the expectation that the business will continue into the future, as opposed to it being a one-off venture.

6.3 The matching (accruals) principle

Revenues and profits should be matched with costs incurred in generating them. This requires that all revenues and expenses are included when they become due — not when they are received or paid.

6.4 The materiality principle

Under this principle, insignificant data (i.e. minor items) can be ignored when constructing accounts.

6.5 Objectivity

Accounts should be drawn up using rules and regulations that avoid the need for personal judgements.

6.6 The prudence or objectivity principle

Revenues and/or profits should never be anticipated in the accounts of a business. They should be included in the profit and loss account only when they are certain.

7 Limitations of published accounts

7.1 Profit and loss accounts

Two themes can be considered in relation to profit and loss accounts.

First, it is easy to assume that a rising level of net or operating profit is evidence of a company that is performing well, and that a falling level implies a company that is struggling. But there are a number of factors that need to be considered when making such a judgement:

- Is the company incurring costs that may enhance its future prospects? For example, it may be restructuring to improve its efficiency but at considerable short-term cost, or it may be investing in training.
- Is a company that pollutes the environment, uses materials from unsustainable sources, but makes a large profit, a successful business?
- Is profit actually the best measure of the performance of a business? Consider government agencies such as social services or charities in this respect.

Secondly, even if we assume that current profits are a good indication of how a company is doing, there are still other issues that must be considered:

- Is the market growing or declining?
- Are new competitors coming on to the scene?
- Is the profit earned likely to be sustained into the future, i.e. is the profit of good quality?

Unfortunately, the financial information in company accounts tells us none of the above.

7.2 Balance sheets

You should be aware of several main aspects concerning balance sheets.

- **A balance sheet is just a 'snapshot' on one day of the year.** If interested parties are examining the accounts several months in the future, the information may be totally out of date.
- The assumption is often made that because a company possesses thousands or millions of pounds worth of assets it is doing well. However, the key issue is *how* the company has financed the purchasing of these assets. A business may present a stable position, but the company may face severe problems if it has borrowed heavily and a rise in interest rates occurs.
- **Importance must be placed on the short-term asset structure of the company.** Many profitable companies close down or go into liquidation, not through lack of sales or customers but through poor management of short-term assets. Effective management of cash flow is essential but is not revealed by examining either profit and loss accounts or balance sheets.
- **External considerations** must also be examined, such as the state of the market or economy, the quality of management and skills of the workforce, and similar-sized organisations in the same industry.

Examiner's tip

It is vital to understand not only the concepts that make up this area of the specification, but also their strengths and weaknesses. Many analytical and evaluative questions are set on the uses and drawbacks of the major financial techniques, so this aspect of understanding is particularly worthwhile.

8 Working capital and liquidity

Working capital refers to the amount of funds a firm has available for its day-to-day operations. It is the amount of liquid assets that a company has available. **Liquidity** measures the extent to which a business is able to pay its short-term debts.

8.1 Working capital

Working capital is an important measure of a business's liquidity and is given by the formula:

working capital = current assets − current liabilities

Working capital is used to pay for the day-to-day running costs of the firm, such as wages, and to finance the purchasing of replacement stocks. It is also used to fund any sales made on credit terms.

Businesses must ensure that they do not have too many current assets in the form of stock and debtors. Conversely, they must make sure that they have enough stock to meet customer requirements.

If a business has too little working capital available, it may struggle to finance its day-to-day operations. Similarly, if it has too much invested in stock or held by debtors, it may not be able to afford to purchase new fixed assets.

8.2 Liquidity

Liquidity is an important concept in business studies. It measures two factors:
* **The ability of a firm to meet its short-term debts**, as suppliers' bills and expenses can only be met with cash. Liquidity in this sense measures the company's cash or near-cash equivalents as against short-term debts.
* **The ability of a business to turn its assets into cash.** Cash or near-cash equivalents (e.g. bank deposits and debtors) are termed **liquid assets**. Assets that are difficult to turn into cash (e.g. buildings, machinery) are termed **illiquid assets**.

Examiner's tip
This area of finance has very close links with the section on liquidity ratios — that is, the current ratio and the acid test — so these are often examined together (see page 72).

9 Depreciation

Fixed assets have a limited life, even though this could be decades in the case of buildings and some machinery. Instead of charging the full cost of an asset to the year in which it is bought, it is usual to charge some of the cost to each year of the asset's life. This appears as a charge on the profit and loss account and the process is termed **depreciation**. The term **amortisation** is sometimes used when intangible assets such as goodwill are depreciated.

9.1 The causes of depreciation
* **Wear and tear** — through use the asset eventually wears out.
* **Decay** — rust, rot, erosion, etc.
* **Obsolescence** — eventually a machine will be replaced by faster, more efficient models, though the old machine is still in perfect working order. In some industries this can occur quickly.
* **Inadequacy** — an asset is no longer useful due to changes in company size or structure.

- **Time** — some assets, such as patents or leases, have a set legal lifetime and therefore lose value as time passes. This process is also known as **amortisation**.
- **Depletion** — some natural assets, such as those which are quarried or mined, run out. They can therefore be depreciated in value.

Some assets may well increase in value rather than decrease. This is called **appreciation**. Normal accounting practice is to ignore this, as it is very subjective. For example, some people may consider that a painting is worth £30 million, while others think it is worthless.

9.2 The straight-line method of depreciation

This is the simplest method of depreciation. It reduces the book value of the asset by the same amount each year over the asset's useful life. It is measured by:

$$\frac{\text{cost of asset} - \text{expected residual (scrap) value}}{\text{useful life in years}} = \text{depreciation charge per year}$$

For example, a machine costs £10,000 and has an anticipated life of 4 years, after which the company hopes to sell it for £4,000.

$$\frac{£10,000 - £4,000}{4} = £1,500 \text{ per year}$$

This is a simple method and is useful when the business is expecting constant returns over the life of an asset.

9.3 The reducing balance method of depreciation

This method of depreciation (also known as the **declining balance method**) reduces the book value of a fixed asset by greater amounts in the earlier years of its operation. This means that the proportion of the cost of the fixed asset included as a cost is greatest in the first year of the asset's life and declines steadily thereafter. In Table 2.4, the reducing balance method writes off a fixed percentage (50%) of the value of the asset in each trading period.

Year	Opening book value	Depreciation (50%)	Closing book value
1	£48,000	£24,000	£24,000
2	£24,000	£12,000	£12,000
3	£12,000	£6,000	£6,000
4	£6,000	£3,000	£3,000

Table 2.4 An example of reducing balance depreciation

The reducing balance method requires that a residual value is estimated and a life for the asset determined. A percentage figure must then be determined which will reduce the value of the asset to the agreed figure over the appropriate number of trading periods. This can be a tricky calculation. However, the reducing balance method is a more accurate approach than the straight-line method, as assets do not lose an equal amount of value in each trading period. In reality, assets lose most of their value in the early years of their life.

10 Window-dressing accounts

Window dressing is presenting company accounts in such a manner as to enhance the financial position of the company. It is sometimes termed **creative accounting** and involves

1.2 Financial efficiency

Activity ratios measure how efficiently an organisation uses its resources. These are sometimes referred to as **asset utilisation ratios**.

1.2a Asset turnover

$$\text{asset turnover} = \frac{\text{sales}}{\text{net assets}}$$

This figure is normally calculated on an annual basis. The ratio measures the efficiency of the use of net assets in generating sales. An increasing ratio result when compared with previous years indicates increasing efficiency. It can usefully be compared with those of competitors.

1.2b Stock turnover

$$\text{stock turnover} = \frac{\text{cost of goods sold}}{\text{average stock held}}$$

This ratio calculates the number of times stock is sold and replaced. It can only really be interpreted with knowledge of the industry in which the firm operates. For example, if we were examining the accounts of a second-hand car sales business, we might expect it to turn over its entire stock of cars and replace them with new ones about once a month. Therefore, we would see a result of 12 times. A greengrocer would expect to sell his stock much more frequently.

As usual, we can undertake a comparison with previous years or other similar-sized firms in the same market. As a general rule, a higher rate of stock turnover (and therefore a higher result) is better. The quicker a business is selling its stock, the quicker it will realise the profit on it.

1.3 Liquidity

Liquidity ratios investigate the short-term and long-term financial stability of the firm by examining the **relationships between assets and liabilities**. These are sometimes also called **solvency ratios**.

1.3a Current ratio

current ratio = current assets : current liabilities

It is generally accepted that an 'ideal' current ratio is approximately 2:1, i.e. £2 of assets for every £1 of debt or liability. This is because some current assets are stock, which can be difficult to convert into cash. The acid test ratio overcomes this by excluding stock.

1.3b Acid test ratio

acid test = (current assets – stock) : current liabilities

Again, conventional wisdom states that an 'ideal' result for this ratio should be approximately 1.1:1, indicating that the organisation has £1.10 to pay every £1.00 of debt. The company can, therefore, pay all its debts and has a 10% safety margin as well. A result below this, e.g. 0.8:1, indicates that the firm may have difficulties meeting short-term payments. Some businesses, however, are able to operate with a very low level of liquidity. Supermarkets, for example, can do so because they do not offer customers credit, and income flows into the business immediately a sale is made.

1.4 Shareholders' ratios

These are also termed **investment ratios**. This group of ratios is concerned with analysing the returns for shareholders. These examine the relationship between the number of shares issued, dividend paid, value of shares and company profits.

1.4a Dividend per share

$$\text{dividend per share (in pence)} = \frac{\text{total dividends}}{\text{number of issued ordinary shares}}$$

1.4b Dividend yield

$$\text{dividend yield (\%)} = \frac{\text{ordinary share dividend (in pence)}}{\text{market price (in pence)}} \times 100$$

Again, a higher result is better. However, the result would once more need to be compared with previous and competitor results as well as any other companies being considered for investment purposes.

1.5 Gearing

Gearing examines the relationship between internal sources and external sources of finance: that is, it compares the amount of capital raised by selling shares with the amount raised through loans.

Gearing is often included in the classification of liquidity ratios, as this ratio focuses on the long-term financial stability of an organisation. It measures the proportion of capital employed by the business that is provided by long-term lenders as against the proportion that has been invested by the owners. In this way, we can see how much of an organisation has been financed by debt. It is given by the formula:

$$\text{gearing (\%)} = \frac{\text{long-term liabilities} + \text{preference shares}}{\text{total capital employed}} \times 100$$

Once again, this is expressed as a percentage.

$$\text{total capital} = \text{ordinary share capital} + \text{preference share capital} + \text{reserves} + \text{debentures} + \text{long-term loans}$$

$$\text{long-term liabilities} = \text{long-term loans} + \text{debentures}$$

The gearing ratio shows the degree of risk involved in investing in a company. If borrowed funds comprise more than 50 % of capital employed, the company is considered to be highly geared. Such a company has to pay interest on its borrowing before it can pay dividends to shareholders or reinvest profits. Companies with lower gearing (those below 50%) offer a lower-risk investment and should find it easier to borrow extra funds if necessary.

Examiner's tip

Concentrate on both learning the ratios and interpreting them, particularly with regard to *improving* the result. No one is going to ask you how you would make a company's performance worse!

2 Limitations of ratio analysis

Although ratio analysis is a powerful tool, it does have several drawbacks:
- It is **retrospective** — ratio analysis concentrates on past performance and is not forward looking. Changes in factors such as the external environment mean that the results of analysing a firm's history may not prove to be a good guide to future performance.
- **Different companies may use different accounting policies**, making true comparison difficult.
- Ratio analysis provides **no information about non-financial matters**, such as the state of the market, the morale of the workforce and the experience of management.
- Ratio analysis **does not take into account the effect inflation may have** on reported figures, especially sales.
- **Comparing like with like** — it is very difficult to find two companies that are exactly the same in terms of size, product mix and objectives.

E Investment decision making

In business studies, investment has two main meanings:
- buying another business
- buying a certain fixed asset

Investment decisions involve risk — resources are to be risked in a venture that may (or may not) bring rewards.

In this section we are concerned with whether or not to purchase a fixed asset. We will further assume that the business is profit maximising — it will choose the item of equipment that provides the highest return on the initial investment rather than one that is more ecologically sound.

Forecasting future returns can be a very difficult, and often expensive, exercise. In many cases, companies are attempting to take decisions about investment projects based on inaccurate data.

The state of the economy plays a major role in determining whether or not a firm undertakes a project. Companies that operate in a stable economic environment can forecast into the future much more easily, as they have confidence that their predictions on the rate of inflation, rate of interest, level of unemployment and hence demand are as accurate as possible.

1 Quantitative appraisal

There are two major considerations when deciding whether or not to invest in a fixed asset:

- the total profits earned by the fixed assets over the asset's useful life
- how quickly the asset will pay off its cost

The process of assessing these factors is called **investment appraisal**. This term refers to the process of comparing two or more potential investments. There are four main methods:

- payback
- average rate of return
- net present value
- internal rate of return

1.1 Payback

Payback quite simply means the number of years it takes to recover the cost of an investment from its earnings.

Example

A machine is bought for £10,000. The purchaser makes an estimate of the additional revenue for each year that will be generated as a result of using the machine and the annual direct and maintenance costs required to support this revenue.

	£
Sales	20,000
Less:	
Direct labour	5,000
Direct materials	6,000
Indirect labour	700
Maintenance	300
Extra income	8,000

If the machine cost £10,000, the investment will pay for itself in 1.25 years. This is found by using the formula:

number of full years + (amount of cost left/revenue generated in next year)

£8,000 = additional revenue generated in 1 year, so amount left to pay = £2,000; revenue generated in next year = £8,000.
So: 1 + (2,000/8,000) = 1.25 years.

This technique is quick and simple but ignores the timing of payments and receipts.

1.2 Average rate of return

This calculates the percentage rate of return on each asset as follows:

$$\frac{\text{average annual profit}}{\text{asset's initial cost}} \times 100$$

$$\text{average profit} = \frac{\text{total net profit before tax over the asset's lifetime}}{\text{useful life of asset}}$$

Example

Machine A will make a profit of £200,000 over 5 years and cost £100,000.

Total profit over 5 years   =   £200,000

Average annual profit   =   £200,000/5

=   £40,000

Average rate of return   = $\dfrac{£40,000}{£100,000} \times 100 = 40\%$

The average rate of return is considered to be more useful than payback because it pays attention to varying cash flow. The final figure should be compared with the rate of interest.

1.3 Net present value

Both payback and the average rate of return method fail to take into account that cash in the hand now is worth more than cash received in the future.

Discounted cash flow converts future earnings from an investment into their present values. These present values are then added up and the cost of the investment subtracted from the total. What remains (if anything) is the **net present value** (NPV). NPV must be positive for the investment to be worthwhile.

Example

An investor deposits £1,000 in a savings account. In return, the bank pays a rate of interest. If the rate of interest is 10%, at the end of 1 year the investment will be worth £1,100.

After 2 years: (£1,100 + 10%) = £1,210
And after 3 years: (£1,210 + 10%) = £1,331

At the end of 3 years, the investor has £1,331 that was only worth £1,000 3 years ago. Looked at in another way, the current or present value of £1,331 in 3 years' time is £1,000. This is because (assuming an interest rate of 10%) the £1,000 can be invested now to be worth £1,331 in 3 years.

To save us having to perform endless repetitive calculations that have been done time and time before, **discounted cash flow tables** are available which relate rates of interest to a period of time in years. An example is given below.

Example

An investment project costs £6,000. The rate of interest is 10% and the project will yield returns for 5 years of £1,800 per year.

Year	Cash flow		Discounting factors (from table)		Present value
0	6,000	×	1.00	=	(6,000)
1	1,800	×	0.909	=	1,636.20
2	1,800	×	0.826	=	1,486.80
3	1,800	×	0.751	=	1,351.80
4	1,800	×	0.683	=	1,229.40
5	1,800	×	0.621	=	1,117.80
				Net present value =	£822.00

If the resulting figure is positive, the investment project is worthwhile. If the result is negative, the project should not be undertaken. A high figure is preferred to a lower one. This has valuable links with the external environment, as obviously the interest rate set by the Bank of England will affect investment decisions (see page 153).

1.4 The internal rate of return

The internal rate of return (IRR) is the rate of discount that is just sufficient to make the net present value of the cash flows associated with a project equal to zero. In the example above we assumed a rate of discount of 10%, which produced a net present value equal to £822. A figure of approximately 11% would be sufficient to make the return equal to zero. Thus the internal rate of return would be 11%.

The IRR can be compared to the rate of interest. This allows a business considering an investment to contrast the likely cost of raising loan capital with the expected return from a project, expressed in present-day values.

2 *Qualitative factors*

As part of their investment decisions, organisations consider other influences such as the effects on industrial relations, the likely reactions of competitors and the degree of risk involved in the decision.

Examiner's tip

When responding to questions on investment appraisal, you should take into account non-financial factors such as those mentioned above. This may be particularly helpful in developing balanced answers and gaining marks for the skill of application.

Ideas for application

Qualitative factors may be the key to earning application marks when tackling evaluative questions on whether or not a firm should invest in a particular project. Try to develop a non-financial theme (e.g. the likely reaction of the workforce) from the case study or scenario to support an argument.

This chapter covers the essential elements of people and organisations. It considers the major theories relating to the motivation of workers, motivation techniques employed by businesses, the styles of leadership available to managers, and the structures adopted by organisations in their attempts to improve performance. The chapter looks at communication, its importance to businesses and how it might be improved. Finally, it covers all aspects of human resource management as well as industrial relations, trade unions and related organisations.

People are important to businesses for many reasons. As we saw in Chapter 1, they are consumers of the goods and services provided by organisations. Without people to purchase their products, firms would not survive. However, organisations also employ people to supply the required goods and services. A business's workforce is a valuable asset that has to be managed effectively. This interaction is shown in Figure 3.1.

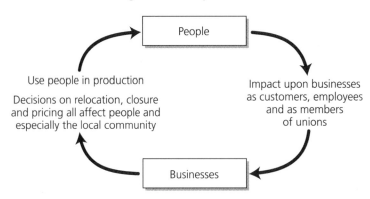

*Figure 3.1
The interaction
between people
and businesses*

AS People and organisations

The AS specification for people and organisations introduces a number of concepts that are vital in business studies, notably motivation and leadership. Although these are part of the AS specification, they are topics that can be used to respond to questions in A2 Business Studies. Other important topics at AS include organisational structure, delegation and consultation. AQA, Edexcel and OCR all have similar content for their A/AS people and organisations specifications, although these are divided up differently between AS and A2 sections. The chart on pages 202–206 sets out these differences in detail.

A Motivation

1 What is motivation?

Writers disagree on the precise meaning of this term. Motivation can be defined as **the will to work due to enjoyment of the work itself**. This suggests that motivation comes from within an individual employee. A different view of motivation is that it is **the will or desire to achieve a given target or goal, due to some external stimuli**. Many of the differences in the theories of motivation can be explained in terms of this fundamental difference of definition. Figure 3.2 shows the various schools of thought relating to motivation.

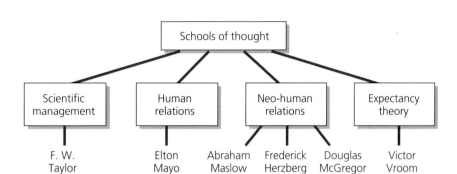

Figure 3.2 Schools of thought relating to motivation

2 Theories of motivation

2.1 The school of scientific management

The first writings on motivating employees emerged in the latter stages of the nineteenth century. Motivating workers became an important issue as the size of organisations increased and as the factory system became firmly entrenched as the core of the manufacturing process. The development of mass production methods increased the number of people working in factories while making their tasks more routine and monotonous. It therefore became an important element of the duties of management to motivate employees so as to improve competitiveness.

A school of thought is simply a group of people who hold broadly similar views. The school of scientific management argues that **business decisions should be taken on the basis of data that are researched and tested quantitatively**. Members of the school believe that it is vital to identify ways in which costs can be accounted for precisely, so that efficiency can be improved. This school of thought supports the use of techniques such as **cost accounting and work-study**.

One of the best-known members of the school of scientific management is **F. W. Taylor** (1856–1915). Taylor was a highly successful engineer who began to advise and lecture on management practices and became a consultant to Henry Ford. His theories were based on a simple interpretation of human behaviour, but some of his methods have survived across the years.

Taylor's ideas were formulated during his time at the Bethlehem Steel Company in the USA. He believed in firm management based on scientific principles, reflecting his background as an engineer. He used a stopwatch to measure how long various activities took and sought the most efficient methods of completing tasks. He then detailed 'normal' times in which duties should be completed, and assessed individual performance against these. Efficiency, he argued, would improve productivity, competitiveness and profits. This required employees to be organised, closely supervised and paid piece rate (according to how much they produced).

Taylor believed that people were 'economic animals' and solely motivated by money. Workers should have no control over their work and the social aspect of employment was considered irrelevant and ignored.

Taylor's views were unpopular with shop-floor employees and resulted in many strikes. As workers and managers became more highly educated, they sought other ways of motivating and organising employees.

3.1e Quality circles

Quality circles are in widespread use to allow employees an opportunity to contribute to decision making. These are small groups of fewer than 20 people who meet regularly to discuss and solve production problems. The members are usually drawn from all levels and areas within the organisation. This ensures that all perspectives are considered. As well as motivating staff, such a group can provide businesses with some valuable ideas. This technique was first used at the Toyota Motor Company in Japan in the 1950s. It has been increasingly adopted in the West since the 1980s.

3.1f Job design and redesign

Many theorists have argued that jobs need to be designed or redesigned with the major motivational factors in mind. They should not be too highly specialised and should offer a varied range of duties. Equally, jobs need to allow people to use their initiative as well as enable them to meet their social needs by working with others.

3.1g Single status

Single status occurs where a business has removed all the barriers that distinguish between various grades of staff. These forms of distinction may include:
- canteens and other social facilities
- different pay systems (salaries versus piece-rate)
- different clothing (managers wearing suits and shop-floor workers wearing overalls)

Removing these barriers is intended to eliminate the 'them and us' attitude that is common in business. The concept of single status originated in Japan but now operates worldwide.

3.2 Financial methods of motivation

Some writers, such as Herzberg, believe that money is not a positive motivator, although the lack of it can demotivate. However, pay systems are nevertheless designed to motivate employees through money.

3.2a Piece-rate pay

Piece-rate pay gives a payment for each item produced. This system encourages effort, but often at the expense of quality. Piece rate is common in agriculture and the textile industry but is difficult to apply in service industries.

3.2b Commission

Commission is a payment made to employees based on the value of sales achieved. It can form all or part of a salary package.

3.2c Profit-related pay

Profit-related pay gives employees a share of the profits earned by the business. This is an approach adopted by the John Lewis Partnership. It encourages all employees to work hard to generate the maximum profits for the business. It also offers firms some flexibility: for example, in less prosperous times, wages can fall along with profits, so reducing the need for redundancies.

3.2d Performance-related pay

Performance-related pay is a topical but controversial technique used in many industries from textiles to education. It needs to be tied into some assessment or appraisal of employee performance. Whatever criteria are used to decide who should receive higher pay, the effect can be divisive and damaging to employee morale.

3.2e Share ownership

Employees are sometimes offered shares in the company in which they work. ASDA operates such a scheme. Shares can be purchased through savings schemes: for example, by shop-floor employees putting aside a few pounds each week. However, share ownership may cause discontentment if this perk is available only to the senior staff.

3.2f Share options

Some businesses offer senior managers and some other employees share options. These are the opportunity to purchase shares in the company at some future date and an agreed price. The employee will take up this option only if the share price is higher than the agreed price when the date arrives. It is hoped that employees will work hard to improve the business's performance (and its share price). If this happens, employees may be able to sell their shares and make an immediate profit.

B Leadership

1 *How to become a leader*

Leaders have authority that has been delegated to them by the organisation. Acceptance of a leader's power by the staff can result from a number of factors:

- **Tradition.** In many long-established firms, senior management posts are handed down from generation to generation in the same family. Members of the next generation of owners are accepted in senior positions irrespective of their ability to do the job.
- **The way a person was appointed.** If the process of selection is seen to be fair, the outcome will be generally supported.
- Some leaders derive their authority from **charisma** and lead others purely by the strength of their personality. Such leaders can develop tremendous loyalty among their staff.

2 What makes a good leader?

A good leader has a number of qualities. Although the exact list might be debatable, the necessary qualities may include:

- a positive self-image and associated self-confidence
- being informed and knowledgeable
- having the ability to think creatively and innovatively
- having the ability to act quickly and decisively
- possessing an air of authority
- first-class communication skills (including listening)
- being able to solve problems, often under pressure

A leader differs from a manager. A manager sets objectives and seeks the most efficient use of resources. A leader motivates people and brings the best out of individuals in pursuit of agreed objectives. These skills could help managers to carry out their duties.

3 Styles of leadership

Some writers on leadership have argued that leaders are born. This is known as **trait theory**. They attempt to identify the features of personality that one would expect to find in a good leader. These are similar to the list above.

Others have rejected this view and contend that people can be taught to be good leaders. This school of thought gives a central role to training in successful leadership.

In spite of the above dispute, four basic categories of leadership style are used widely for purposes of analysis. These are **democratic**, **paternalistic**, **authoritarian** and **laissez-faire**. Each style has advantages and disadvantages, and each is perhaps appropriate in particular circumstances (see Table 3.1).

> **Examiner's tip**
>
> Democratic leadership is not always the best style. It is important to relate the style of leadership to the circumstances. The factors below would influence the style of management selected.

The **style of management** required might depend upon:

- **The culture of the business.** If employees are used to autocratic management, preparation and (especially) training will be required before a change of style.
- **The nature of the task.** For example, a complex and lengthy task is more likely to require democratic management.
- **The nature of the workforce.** Less skilled and large groups of employees might be more likely to respond to autocratic styles of management. The personalities and potential of the workforce will also influence the style of leadership adopted.
- **The personality and skills of the leader.** Good communication and other interpersonal skills might encourage democratic leadership. Alternatively, high levels of knowledge of the task may encourage a more autocratic approach.

Tannenbaum and Schmidt developed this idea further. They argued that the style of leadership depends upon the prevailing circumstances. Leaders should have the ability to exercise a range of leadership styles and should deploy them as appropriate. Therefore, a good leader has the necessary talents to adapt his or her style to the circumstances. Table 3.2 illustrates the range of styles a leader might use.

Type/features	Democratic	Paternalistic	Authoritarian	Laissez faire
Description	Democratic leadership entails running a business on the basis of decisions agreed by the majority.	The paternalistic approach is dictatorial, but decisions are intended to be in the best interests of the employees.	An authoritarian leadership style keeps information and decision making among the senior managers.	Laissez-faire leadership means the leader has a peripheral role, leaving staff to manage the business.
Key features	Encourages participation and makes use of delegation.	Leader explains decisions and ensures social and leisure needs are met.	Sets objectives and allocates tasks. Leader retains control through-out.	Leader evades duties of management and uncoordinated delegation occurs.
Communication	Extensive, two-way. Encourages contributions from subordinates.	Generally downwards, though feedback will take place.	One-way communication, downwards from leader to subordinate.	Mainly horizontal communication, though little communication occurs.
Uses	When complex decisions are made requiring a range of specialist skills.	Can appear democratic, but is really 'soft' autocracy.	Useful when quick decisions are required.	Can encourage production of highly creative work by subordinates.
Advantages	Commitment to business, satisfaction and quality of work may all improve.	Can engender loyalty, and frequently enjoys low labour turnover due to emphasis on social needs.	Decisions and direction of business will be consistent. May project image of confident, well-managed business.	May bring best out of highly professional or creative groups.
Disadvantages	Slow decision making and need for consensus may avoid taking 'best' decisions.	Really autocratic and can result in groups becoming highly dependent. They may become dissatisfied with leader.	Lack of information so subordinates highly dependent upon leaders; supervision needed.	May not be deliberate, but bad management — staff lack focus and sense of direction. Much dissatisfaction.

Table 3.1 Leadership styles

Use of authority by the leader					
				Degree of freedom enjoyed by subordinates	
Tells	**Sells**	**Tests**	**Consults**	**Joins**	**Delegates**
Leader Owns and resolves total problem and instructs subordinates.	Leader Resolves problem and informs subordinates.	Leader Tackles problem but seeks opinions.	Leader Proposes alternatives and seeks recommend-ations.	Leader Works together with subordinates in taking decisions.	Leader Passes authority to subordinates for decision making.
Subordinate Simply responds.	Subordinate Receives explanation and acts.	Subordinate Expresses views on decision.	Subordinate Discusses alternatives and gives recommend-ations.	Subordinate Helps shape objectives and solutions. Views accepted.	Subordinate Exercises authority and owns the decisions taken.

Table 3.2 Tannenbaum and Schmidt's continuum of leadership behaviour

One of the dilemmas faced by leaders is **the tension between the needs of people and the needs of the task**. Some of the facets of democratic leadership, such as two-way communication, may be difficult to enact in circumstances in which a task has to be completed in a short time. On the other hand, leaders who focus on the task may damage the morale of colleagues and the efficiency of the organisation by not involving colleagues. This dilemma reinforces the view that there is no single 'best' style of leadership and that approaches appropriate to the circumstances should be adopted.

Ideas for application

Leadership styles may vary according to the circumstances. The appropriate method will depend upon the personality of the leader, the ability and skills of the workforce and the timescale. Try to develop themes such as these in an answer on leadership styles.

4 *Delegation and consultation*

Delegation can be defined as the passing of authority to a subordinate within the organisation. Although a task may be passed down from a superior to a subordinate, the manager still has the responsibility for making sure that the job is completed. On the other hand, **authority is the ability to carry out the task. It is possible to delegate authority, but responsibility remains with the delegator.**

To delegate, a manager must trust the delegatee and it is important that the subordinate feels that trust is placed in him or her. A prudent manager would also want to exercise some control over the subordinate — for example, via reports and inspections. Any increase in control exercised by the manager decreases the amount of trust enjoyed by the subordinate. To give more trust involves a release of some control. The advantages and disadvantages of delegation are outlined in Table 3.3.

Advantages	Disadvantages
• Delegation and trust are cheap — they free seniors for other (strategic) matters.	• Trusting subordinates can be risky and responsibility remains with the senior.
• Delegation may also breed a sense of responsibility.	• Controlling subordinates is safe in that abuse is avoided.
• Controlling subordinates is expensive.	• Delegation requires (expensive) training for subordinates.
• Delegation allows specialisation.	
• Delegation allows individuals to develop skills and careers.	• Once trust is given, it is impossible to withdraw it without loss of face.
• Without delegation there is no training for prospective managers.	• Trust is fragile: once broken it is never the same.
• Too little delegation leads to senior managers overworking.	

Table 3.3 Delegation — the balance sheet

Other points worth noting are that it is easier for managers to trust subordinates if they have done the job themselves and if they select the subordinate. In addition, the degree of delegation used in any circumstances depends upon:
- the skill and experience of managers and subordinates
- the degree of risk to which the business is exposed
- the company philosophy — is delegation commonly used?

5 Centralisation and decentralisation

Centralisation occurs when the majority of decisions are the responsibility of just a few people at the top of the organisation. In many senses, centralisation is the opposite of delegation.

Decentralisation occurs when control has shifted sideways or horizontally (between people at the same level in the organisation), while **delegation** implies a downward shift in control. **Decentralisation is not the same as delegation but is often accompanied by it.**

Examiner's tip

Delegation is an important element of many responses, particularly those requiring analysis and evaluation. It may be a key component of arguments relating to implementation of teamworking, empowerment, etc. This can be a key part of developing an analytical line of argument. It is important to recognise that this approach has advantages and disadvantages and that a well-balanced answer will reflect this.

C Organisational structures

1 Functional and matrix structures

Businesses can organise themselves internally in a number of ways. The two main structures are:
- functional
- matrix

1.1 Functional structures

An organisational structure that is functional is illustrated in Figure 3.6.

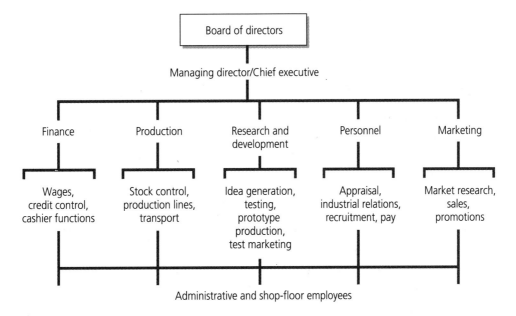

Figure 3.6 A functional structure

1.1a Advantages of a functional structure

- It allows the business to be coordinated from the top and to have a sense of overall direction.
- It provides clear lines of communication and authority for all employees.
- It lets specialists operate in particular areas, such as marketing and research and development, and to develop new and innovative ideas.

1.1b Disadvantages of a functional structure

- Senior managers may become very remote as the business grows and may become unaware of local issues.
- Decision making may be slow because of long lines of communication, which may damage competitiveness.
- It provides little coordination and direction to those lower in the organisation.

1.2 Matrix structures

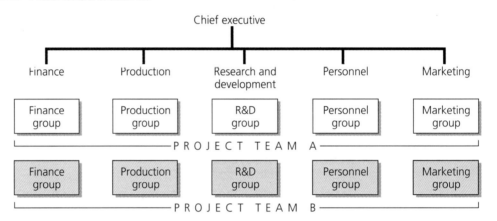

Figure 3.7 A matrix structure

The **matrix structure** (see Figure 3.7) was first used in the USA and has become more popular in the UK. This type of structure combines the traditional departments seen in Figure 3.6 with project teams. For example, a project or task team established to develop a new product might include engineers and design specialists as well as those with marketing, financial, personnel and production skills. These teams can be temporary or permanent depending on the tasks they are asked to complete. Each team member can end up with two or more **line managers** — their normal **departmental manager** as well as the **manager of the project**.

1.2a Advantages of a matrix structure

- It can help to break down traditional department barriers, improving communication across the entire organisation.
- It can allow individuals to use particular skills in a variety of contexts.
- It avoids the need for several departments to meet regularly, so reducing costs and improving coordination.

1.2b Disadvantages of a matrix structure

- Members of project teams may have divided loyalties, as they report to two or more line managers. Equally, this scenario can put project team members under a heavy pressure of work.
- There may not be a clear line of accountability for project teams, given the complex nature of matrix structures.

2 Levels of hierarchy and spans of control

The levels of hierarchy refer to the **number of layers within an organisation**. Traditional organisations were tall, with many layers of hierarchy, and were often authoritarian in nature. Figure 3.8 shows an organisation with four levels of hierarchy. We consider levels of hierarchy in more detail in the next section.

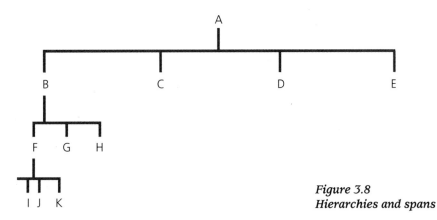

Figure 3.8
Hierarchies and spans

The **span of control** is the number of subordinates for whom a manager is directly responsible. In Figure 3.8 manager A has a span of control of four, because he or she is **not** directly responsible for employees F, G, H, I, J and K. Employee B has a span of control of three. The **maximum recommended span for effective management is six**, though this is regularly exceeded, particularly in recent years. The span of control in operation will depend upon a number of factors:

- **The experience and personality of the manager.**
- **The nature of the business.** If being a line manager requires a great deal of close supervision, a narrower span might be appropriate.
- **The skills and attitudes of the employees.** Highly skilled, professional employees might flourish in a business adopting wide spans of control.
- **The tradition and culture of the organisation.** A business with a tradition of democratic management and empowered workers may operate wider spans of control.

3 Delayering organisations

Many businesses in the manufacturing and service sectors have moved towards flatter organisational structures through delayering. **Delayering involves removing one or more levels of hierarchy from the organisational structure.** This idea crossed the Atlantic from the United States.

Frequently, the layers removed are those containing middle managers. For example, many high-street banks no longer have a manager in each of their branches, preferring to appoint a manager to oversee a number of branches.

3.1 Advantages of delayering

- It offers opportunities for delegation, empowerment and motivation, as the number of managers is reduced and more authority is given to shop-floor workers.
- It can improve communication within the organisation, as messages have to pass through fewer levels of hierarchy.
- It can remove departmental rivalry if department heads are removed and the workforce is organised in teams.
- It can reduce costs, as fewer employees are required and employing middle managers can be expensive.

3.2 Disadvantages of delayering

- Not all organisations are suited to flatter organisational structures — mass production industries with low-skilled employees may not adapt easily.
- Delayering can have a negative impact on motivation due to job losses, especially if it is really just an excuse for redundancies.
- Initial disruption may occur as people take on new responsibilities and fulfil new roles.
- Those managers remaining will have a wider span of control, which, if it is too wide, can damage communication within the business.

4 Line and staff responsibilities

Line managers normally hold departmental responsibilities (including managing people and other resources) and derive their title from fulfilling a role in the line of command from the top to the bottom of the hierarchy. They carry out their duties with the aim of assisting the business in meeting its corporate objectives.

Staff managers are often appointed as the organisation grows in size and are used to relieve senior managers of some time-consuming duties, such as personnel and marketing. They are appointed to offer support and contribute only indirectly towards achieving corporate objectives. Line managers do not always welcome the appointment of specialist staff managers. They might feel that their positions and status are threatened, and may believe staff managers only understand a part of the complexities of their jobs.

5 Management by objectives

Peter Drucker spent many years researching major companies, such as IBM, and in 1964 published his theory of **management by objectives (MBO)**. This theory highlighted the importance of objectives as a management technique. Under MBO, managers should:
- identify and agree targets for achievement with subordinates
- negotiate the support that will be required to achieve these targets
- evaluate over time the extent to which these objectives are met

The objectives set at each level should be coordinated to ensure that the business achieves its corporate objectives. Each member of staff should make a contribution, no matter how small, towards the whole business meeting its targets.

5.1 Advantages of MBO

- It improves communication within the organisation as the target-setting and evaluation process takes place. It can give managers a fuller appreciation of the

duties and problems faced by their subordinates.

- Employees may be motivated by having a clear understanding of what they are trying to achieve, thus improving performance.
- It can highlight training needs for managers and subordinates, improving their performance and productivity.
- The attainments of goals can help all employees to fulfil some of the higher needs identified by Maslow.

5.2 Disadvantages of MBO

Drucker recognised at the outset that MBO had a number of potential problems.

- Some employees may find the setting of targets threatening. Employees at different levels within the organisation have varying perceptions of issues, problems and their solutions. The manager might set targets that the subordinate considers unachievable.
- All employees within the organisation must be committed to the technique if it is to succeed and benefit the business.
- Setting targets for highly specialised employees can be difficult and tends to remove the focus from the mainstream corporate objectives.

D Human resource management

1 *What is human resource management?*

Human resource management (HRM) entails the use and development of a business's labour force in the most efficient manner. This is an approach to the effective utilisation of people initiated by Japanese companies. HRM is not simply another term for the activities carried out by the personnel department. It involves:

- developing individuals through training, often as part of the appraisal process
- giving managers responsibility for developing and making the best use of the labour force available to them

Some businesses (especially Japanese ones) operate without a personnel department in the belief that the management of people is the duty of all managers.

2 *Planning the workforce*

Planning the most effective use of human resources is an important element in meeting corporate objectives. Businesses have to decide on the amount and type of labour that they will require, given their objectives and the anticipated level of sales. Those responsible for HRM draw up a **workforce plan** to detail the number and type of workers the business needs to recruit as well as any necessary redeployments, redundancies and retraining. The plan also specifies how the business will implement its workforce plan. An important element of this is a **skills audit** to identify the abilities and qualities of the existing workforce, highlighting skills and talents within the workforce of which managers were unaware.

Businesses require specific information for their development of workforce plans (see Figure 3.9):

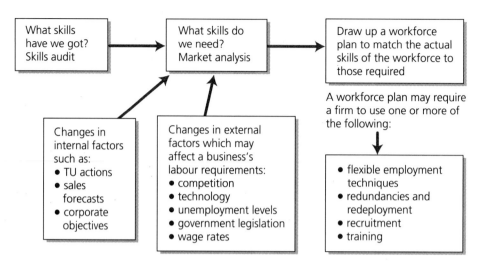

Figure 3.9 Workforce planning

- They need to undertake research to provide sales forecasts for the next year or two. This helps identify the quantity and type of labour the firm will require.
- They need data that show the number of employees likely to be leaving the labour force in general (and the firm in particular). They also need information on potential entrants to the labour force, which depends on demographic factors.
- They need to consider likely wage rates. If wages are expected to rise, then businesses may reduce their demand for labour and seek to make greater use of technology.
- Technological developments will impact on planning the workforce, as they may reduce the need for unskilled or even skilled employees while creating employment for those with technical skills.

A workforce plan will allow the company to use its human resources effectively and at minimum cost in pursuit of its corporate objectives.

3 Recruitment, selection and training

All businesses, even very small ones, need to recruit employees at some stage. The process of recruitment is shown in Figure 3.10.

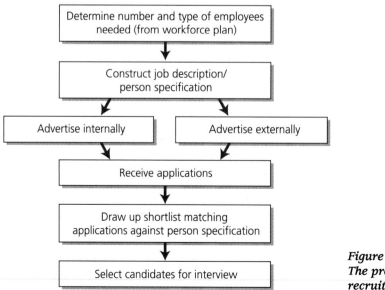

*Figure 3.10
The process of
recruitment*

3.1 Documentation

The personnel department prepares the necessary documentation for the recruitment process.

3.1a Job adverts

Job adverts contain the following information:

- job title
- some description of duties
- location
- name of the business
- possibly salary and working hours

The advert may be local for a relatively unskilled job. Highly skilled and professional positions might require advertising nationally or even internationally.

3.1b Job descriptions

Job descriptions may act as the basis for drawing up the advert for the post and relate to the position rather than the person. Typically, job descriptions contain the following information:

- title of the post
- employment conditions
- some idea of tasks and duties
- to whom employees are responsible
- likely targets and standards that employees are expected to meet

3.1c Person or job specifications

Person or job specifications set out the qualifications and qualities required of an employee. The list might include:

- educational and professional qualifications required
- character and personality traits expected
- physical characteristics needed
- experience necessary

Recruitment can be an expensive exercise but is less costly than appointing the wrong employee and perhaps having to repeat the process.

3.2 Internal and external recruitment

3.2a Internal recruitment

Firms may recruit internally through promotion or redeployment of existing employees. This offers **benefits**:

- It is cheaper, as it avoids the need for expensive external advertising.
- Candidates will have experience of the business and may not require induction training.
- Selection may be easier, as more is known about the candidates.

However, **problems** exist in recruiting internally:

- Selection is from a smaller pool of available labour and the calibre of candidates may be lower. This can be significant for senior appointments.
- Difficulties can result if employees are promoted from within — former colleagues may resent taking orders from those whom they formerly worked alongside.

3.2b External recruitment

Managers may be keen to have a wider choice of candidates and therefore advertise externally. The **advantages** of this approach are as follows:

- It is likely that higher-quality candidates will be available following external recruitment, even if advertisements are only placed in local media.
- External candidates will bring fresh ideas and enthusiasm into the business.

But **drawbacks** exist:

- It is more expensive to recruit externally, especially if national advertising or employment agencies are used.
- The degree of risk is greater, even if extensive selection processes are used, as candidates are less known to the business.

> **Examiner's tip**
> Students sometimes provide huge amounts of information on recruitment and selection. This is a descriptive area and one on which only relatively straightforward questions testing knowledge and understanding are set. Few marks are normally available for such questions. It is more important to appreciate the role of recruitment and selection within the whole HRM process and the influences on this process.

3.3 Selection

Because of the costs involved in recruiting the wrong people, firms are investing more resources and time in the recruitment process. Although effective selection techniques may be expensive, they are considerably cheaper than appointing the wrong employee.

A number of techniques of selection exist:

- **Interviews** remain the most common form of selection and may involve one or two interviewers or even a panel interview. Interviews are relatively cheap and allow the two-way exchange of information, but they are unreliable as a method of selection. Some people perform well at interview, but that does not necessarily mean they will perform well in the post.
- **Psychometric tests** reveal more about the personality of a candidate than might be discovered through interview. Questions are frequently used to assess candidates' management skills or ability to work within a team.
- **Aptitude tests** may provide an insight into a candidate's current ability and potential. Such tests can also be used to assess intelligence and job-related skills.
- **Assessment centres** expose candidates for jobs to a number of methods of selection, including role plays, group activities and simulations of circumstances that might occur in the job. Assessment centres allow a direct comparison between candidates.

3.4 Training

Training entails improving the skills and knowledge of the workforce. Almost all employees receive some training when they commence a particular job. This is known as **induction training**. Induction training is intended to introduce an employee to the business in which they will be working. It may include familiarisation with some or all of the following:

- important policies and procedures, such as appraisal, holiday entitlement, systems and disciplinary/grievance matters
- the layout of the factory or offices
- personnel with whom the new employee will be working
- health and safety and security procedures
- the fundamental duties associated with the job

Induction training offers a number of **advantages** to businesses:
- It enables a new recruit to become more productive more quickly.
- It can prevent costly errors resulting from employee ignorance.
- It may make a new employee feel more welcome and reduce labour turnover.

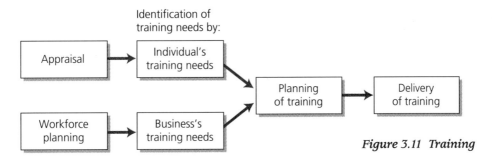

Figure 3.11 Training

There are two broad types of training:
- **Off-the-job.** This is training outside the workplace, either at a college, university or some other training agency, or at the employee's home. Off-the-job training can take the form of external courses, perhaps in the form of lectures and seminars, self-study or open learning.
- **On-the-job.** This form of training does not require the employee to leave the workplace. He or she learns from more experienced employees through observation and work shadowing. Alternatively, the trainee may work through instruction manuals, operate with a mentor or receive more formal guidance from senior employees.

	Off-the-job	On-the-job
Advantages	• Employees not distracted by work pressures. • Specialists can be used to provide training. • Often carries greater conviction with employees.	• Simple to organise and often relatively cheap. • Closely related to the needs and circumstances of the business. • Employees can see relevance of training.
Disadvantages	• Can be costly. • Employees absent from work for period of time. • Can place greater pressures (extra hours, commitment) on other employees. • If general training, employees may leave when complete.	• Those delivering training often do not have teaching or training skills. • Trainees can be distracted by demands of job, e.g. by phone calls. • Training can be narrowly focused, not looking at the broader needs of the organisation.

Table 3.4 The advantages and disadvantages of training

In spite of being expensive, and sometimes disruptive, training does offer organisations **a number of benefits**:
- Well-trained employees are likely to be better motivated, as they feel valued by their employers and get a sense of achievement from performing their work more efficiently or carrying out more complex duties.
- Training improves employee performance, resulting in a more productive and efficient workforce. This can improve the competitiveness of the organisation.
- Training can help to reduce labour turnover as employees are more satisfied with their work. It may also help to make the business more attractive to potential employees.

The government encourages training through its 'Investors in People' scheme. Firms that meet the requirement for training of employees (in particular, for training employees to assist in meeting corporate objectives) are entitled to use a logo identifying them as meeting this particular standard. This may assist the business in its dealings with customers and other businesses. Indeed, some firms will only deal with suppliers if they have the 'Investors in People' award.

Ideas for application

Training can be very important for certain types of business. It can provide differentiation for firms selling similar products and may be especially important for firms operating in service industries to ensure the quality of their service exceeds those of competitors.

A2 People and organisations

This section builds on the material covered at AS. It is recommended that you re-read the AS materials alongside those that follow. Although A2 questions will focus on the following topics, it is likely that some of the principles covered at AS will be needed to support your answers.

A Communication

1 Definition

Communication is the exchange of information between people within and outside organisations. Communication has succeeded when a response (feedback) has been received. Figure 3.12 summarises the various forms of communication.

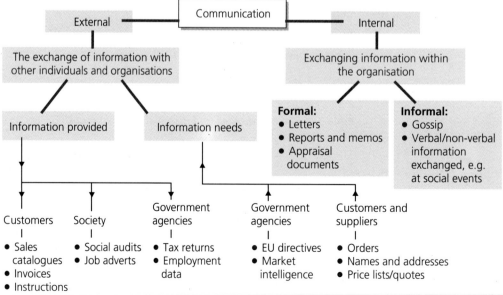

Figure 3.12 A summary of communication

2 *Methods of communication*

2.1 Verbal and non-verbal communication

- **Telephone communication** is widely used in business to transmit simple messages quickly and effectively. It allows contact with individuals and offers immediate feedback.
- **Meetings.** These occur in a variety of forms, including board and shareholder meetings, and meetings with customers and suppliers. Less formal meetings, such as quality circles and social events, are also forums for the exchange of information.
- **Presentations** are frequently used in businesses — internally to transmit information on new projects and ideas, and externally to attract new customers. Many presentations use Microsoft PowerPoint. Detailed information (especially relating to sales and products) can be exchanged using this software.
- **Interviews** are a formal method of communication that may be used to appoint new staff or to deal with disciplinary or grievance issues.
- **Non-verbal communication** includes body language and facial expressions as well as the tone of voice used and the degree of eye contact made by the parties to the communication.

Examiner's tip

While a broad understanding of the methods of communication is important, highly detailed information is not relevant to A-level Business Studies. Examiners will not set questions asking you to describe a number of methods of communication.

2.2 Written communication

This is more appropriate when detailed information needs to be exchanged. It can be slow, though modern technology (e.g. faxes and e-mails) can speed up the process.

- **Reports** are widely used by businesses to transmit information. They can relate to important issues, such as an investigation into the establishment of a new nuclear power station. They are also used to disseminate the financial performance of companies.
- **Business letters** are a major external form of communication used, for example, to place orders with suppliers or to arrange other forms of communication such as meetings.
- **Memoranda** are extensively used within businesses to exchange information concisely and rapidly on a wide range of topics.

2.3 Technology and communication

Developments in technology have transformed the way in which businesses communicate, and some of the developments have as yet unfulfilled potential:

- **Fax (or facsimile) machines** play a key role in transmitting detailed information between businesses through use of the telephone network. They offer a fast and relatively cheap form of communication, ideal for contracts, engineering drawings and drafts of publicity materials.
- **Electronic mail (e-mail).** This method of communication allows computers to speak to one another throughout the world for the cost of a local telephone call. Messages are stored on servers and can be accessed by the recipient through the use of a password. This is particularly useful for quick international communication across different time zones, as messages can be stored until the recipient is available.

The amount of business communication conducted through the medium of e-mail has risen enormously over recent years.

- **The internet.** This is an international electronic communications network, with over 500 million users. It is an unregulated network devoted mostly to communication and research but with many commercial possibilities. It enables large businesses to heighten their profiles and smaller businesses to promote their products to consumers across the globe. Some businesses, such as the Amazon bookshop, owe their success to exploiting the internet. For many smaller businesses, the internet makes it possible to sell products to consumers throughout the world.
- **Intranets.** These are electronic, computer-based communication networks, similar in nature to the internet but used internally by individual businesses. They are ideally suited to large companies, especially those with a number of locations. They provide an e-mail service as well as access to information of interest to large numbers of employees.
- **Video conferencing.** This allows people to communicate face-to-face while in different locations, nationally or internationally. It saves time and avoids the need for employees to travel to meetings.

2.3a Benefits of technology for communication

- It provides a cheap and quick method to communicate and can transfer complex and highly technical information effectively. It is of particular value to companies that operate internationally.
- It avoids the need for endless pieces of paper as businesses strive towards paperless administrative systems.
- It allows automatic generation of communications, such as re-ordering stocks and invoicing customers.

2.3b Disadvantages of technology for communication

- Some employees may be resistant to the new technology and make ineffective use of it.
- New technology can be expensive to install and may require substantial training of employees, incurring further costs.
- High-technology communication systems can generate enormous amounts of communication that may not improve the efficiency of the organisation.
- Although many firms use the internet, it has proved difficult to make acceptable levels of profits from operating on the World Wide Web.

3 Barriers to effective communication

Businesses may encounter a number of factors preventing successful communication:

- Transmitters of information may use terms or jargon that is unfamiliar to recipients, leading to misunderstanding.
- Too much information might be transmitted, causing overload on the part of the recipient.
- A sender of information might choose the wrong medium for communication (e.g. using the telephone to transmit detailed and complex information).
- Sometimes group norms can inhibit communication — some organisations with cultures that keep managers and shop-floor workers separate may incur disadvantages in terms of efficiency.

- Differences in cultures, time zones and languages can all contribute to ineffective communication.
- The provision of incomplete information (perhaps due to time or cost constraints) can inhibit successful communication.
- Some subordinates may be reluctant to give superiors bad news (e.g. the loss of a major customer) and this can prevent effective internal communication.

4 The importance of communication

Effective communication systems are important to all businesses. Often, communication is not given the attention it deserves and many managers underestimate its role within a successful organisation.

- Communication can play an important part in **motivating the workforce**. Encouraging (and listening) to the views and opinions of junior employees, perhaps through feedback, will increase their sense of self-worth and should improve motivation. It may also be the source of some good ideas — for example, through quality circles. Such upward communication is a central element in teamwork and empowerment.
- **Effective internal communication can help to provide greater understanding of differences in cultures and opinions within an organisation.** This may prevent prejudice and rivalries damaging the performance of the business.
- Communication is a means by which **businesses present themselves to society in general and potential customers in particular**. Effective communication — for example, through publicity materials — can present the organisation in a positive light and improve sales. Some businesses spend heavily on corporate advertising rather than promoting individual products.
- **Effective external communication is an essential part of achieving customer satisfaction.** The product must be described and priced accurately, orders must be fulfilled promptly and correctly, and any complaints or questions must be dealt with effectively. Poor (or no) communication is the cause of many criticisms of businesses and their products.

Examiner's tip

This is a fruitful area for questions in A-level Business Studies. You should have a clear understanding of communication and how it relates to motivation, morale and competitiveness. It is important to appreciate that the communication problems experienced by small and large firms are very different. The solutions they may implement are also radically different. Taking this approach will assist you in earning marks for application.

Ideas for application

There are circumstances in which communication is particularly difficult: during periods of growth or at times of crisis. Ironically, it is at these times that communication is most important. Firms need to invest in communication (using training and not just IT) at these times. Answers on communication should recognise times at which communication is especially important to the business in the scenario.

B Human resource management

The A2 material for human resource management builds upon the principles developed earlier in the AS section. HRM is the process of making the most efficient use of an organisation's employees. HRM regards all aspects of managing the workforce as integrated and essential in ensuring that the organisation attains its corporate objectives. Therefore policies relating to recruitment, pay and appraisal should be designed as part of a co-ordinated human resource strategy. Human resource management should be an integrated approach that aims to make the best use of human resources in relation to the business's overall goals.

Some elements of HRM were covered in the AS section of this chapter. These are:
- the notion of workforce planning
- recruitment and selection
- training

In this section we shall consider the approaches that can be taken to human resource management as well as issues such as appraisal, pay systems and the measurement of personnel effectiveness.

1 The attraction of HRM

Since the 1970s many firms have abandoned personnel management in favour of human resource management (HRM). Personnel management encompassed tasks such as recruitment and selection, training, discipline, pay and employee records. This approach viewed each of these tasks as discrete functions and personnel management was not considered to be a strategic function. It was not uncommon for personnel management to be overseen by a middle manager.

The adoption of HRM has elevated the status of people who manage people! Making the most effective use of the workforce has become a strategic function, headed by a senior manager or a director. It also integrates all elements of managing people to ensure that the approach is co-ordinated.

Businesses have adopted HRM for a number of reasons.
- In the western economies, the majority of firms supply services. In service industries the quality of employees is an important competitive weapon. Therefore making the most effective use of the workforce can assist in boosting profits and achieving other corporate objectives.
- Companies using HRM have appeared to manage their workforces more effectively and have become more competitive as a consequence. Other businesses have therefore imitated this approach.
- The process of delayering and the delegation of authority have meant that managers further down the organisational hierarchy have taken more decisions in relation to employees. The philosophy of HRM fits in with this approach.

2 Hard and soft approaches to HRM

Not all businesses take the same view of HRM. Two broad approaches have emerged.
- **'Hard' HRM.** The 'hard' HRM approach views employees as a resource to be used

as efficiently as possible; in this way they are no different from vehicles or production machinery. Employees are hired as cheaply as possible, managed closely and made redundant when no longer required.

- **'Soft' HRM.** The 'soft' approach is based on the belief that employees are perhaps the most valuable asset a business possesses. Thus it is in the business's interest to maximise their value to the organisation. Employees are valued and developed over time and help to make a business competitive in the marketplace.

	'Hard' HRM	**'Soft' HRM**
Philosophy	Employees are no different from any other resource used by the business.	Considers employees to be the most valuable resource available to the business and a vital competitive weapon.
Timescale	HRM operates in the short term only: employees are hired and fired as necessary.	Employees are developed over a long period of time to help the firm fulfil its corporate objectives.
Key features	Pay is kept to a minimum. Little or no empowerment. Communication is mainly downwards. Leaders have theory X view of employees. Emphasis is on the short term in recruiting and training employees.	Employees are empowered and encouraged to take decisions. Leaders have theory Y view of workforce. Employees are encouraged to extend and update skills. Employees are consulted regularly by managers. A long-term relationship is developed with employees through use of internal recruitment and ongoing training programmes.
Associated leadership style	This approach to HRM is more likely to be adopted by leaders using an autocratic style of leadership.	This approach to HRM is more likely to be adopted by leaders using a democratic style of leadership.
Motivational techniques used	Principally financial techniques with minimal use of techniques such as delegation.	Techniques intended to give employees more control over their working lives, e.g. delegation and empowered teams.

Table 3.5 Alternative approaches to HRM

3 Appraisal

In general terms, appraisal is used to assess employee performance. Appraisal usually takes the form of an interview with the individual's line manager, often annually. The appraisal process may be used for a number of reasons:

- It may be an opportunity to review the employee's recent progress, particularly since the previous appraisal.
- It may involve target setting. The individual's performance in pursuit of these targets may form the basis of a future appraisal interview.
- Appraisal interviews are often used to identify an employee's training needs following an evaluation of recent performance.
- It may determine future salaries or promotions.

Two broad types of appraisal exist:

- **Developmental appraisal.** This places the emphasis not so much on an employee's performance as on those factors that might improve it. The appraisal process is designed to identify employees' training needs and to fulfil them in the expectation of improving the business's performance.

- **Judgmental appraisal.** Here, the most important factor is to assess the performance of the employee against some yardstick, perhaps the performance of others or targets set earlier. Those employees deemed to be successful may be rewarded with bonuses, pay rises or promotions.

It could be argued that developmental appraisal systems are more likely to have a positive impact upon motivation by meeting the higher needs of employees or by providing Herzberg's motivators.

4 Pay systems

Employees can be paid using a variety of systems, each of which offers advantages and disadvantages. Some pay systems such as piece rate and commission are more likely to be associated with the 'hard' approach to HRM.

- **Flat rate.** This entails fixed weekly or monthly pay based on an agreed number of hours. It is a simple system to administer but is unlikely to motivate employees.
- **Piece rate.** Here, an agreed payment is made for each item produced. The piece-rate system encourages effort but may reduce quality of output. This system is common in agriculture.
- **Time rate.** Under this system employees receive a given rate per hour up to an agreed number of hours each week. Any hours worked beyond this receive a higher rate of pay (overtime).
- **Bonus.** This is paid as an extra incentive to employees. It is frequently paid out of profits and usually acts as an encouragement to employees during busy trading periods.
- **Commission.** This may be paid as a percentage of the value of sales made by a sales-person. Commission can be part or all of an employee's pay, though it is becoming less common for employees to be paid solely through commission.
- **Profit-related pay.** Under this system employees receive a share of the profits earned by the business employing them. This system grants businesses some flexibility when setting wages: pay can justifiably fall during less prosperous periods. This means that businesses may be less likely to make redundancies.

In a democratically managed company using a 'soft' HRM system and delegating authority, the pay system may be intended to:

- encourage staff to be independent and creative
- produce high-quality products and meet customer needs as fully as possible
- provide solutions to problems and contribute to decision making

In contrast, a more autocratically led organisation may have a radically different pay system. This system might have the following objectives:

- to control the workforce
- to ensure employees complete tasks in agreed ways

Employees who do not conform might lose some part of their pay.

5 Measuring employee performance

Managers need to measure employee performance in an objective way for the following reasons:

- to assess the efficiency (and competitiveness) of the workforce
- to assist in developing the workforce plan
- to confirm that the business's human resource planning is contributing directly to the achievement of the corporate objectives

5.1 The key performance indicators

One of the factors influencing an organisation's workforce plan is the performance of its existing employees. This will highlight the need for training, further recruitment or, perhaps, redundancy or redeployment. There are a number of ways a business can assess the performance of its current labour force.

5.2 Labour productivity

$$\text{labour productivity} = \frac{\text{output per period}}{\text{number of employees at work}} \times 100$$

We look at labour productivity in detail in Chapter 4. If workers are producing a similar or greater amount each day, week or month than employees of rival businesses, then productivity may be satisfactory. However, such comparisons may be simplistic: factors such as wage rates, the level of technology and the way the labour force is organised will also be important.

Examiner's tip
It is important to look behind any labour force data with which you are provided. For example, two sets of productivity data may suggest that firm A has a clear advantage. This may become less clear cut when the following factors relating to firm B are taken into account:
- Wage rates are significantly lower.
- Morale is excellent.
- A training programme is being implemented, causing short-term disruption.
- There is a low incidence of industrial relations problems.
- A reputation for craftsmanship and quality products has been established.

5.3 Labour turnover

$$\text{turnover (\%)} = \frac{\text{number of staff leaving during the year}}{\text{average number of staff}} \times 100$$

A high level of labour turnover could be caused by many factors:
- inadequate wage levels, leading employees to defect to competitors
- poor morale and low levels of motivation within the workforce
- the selection of the wrong employees in the first place, meaning they leave to seek more suitable employment
- a buoyant local labour market offering more (and perhaps more attractive) opportunities to employees

High rates of labour turnover are expensive in terms of additional recruitment costs, lost production costs and the damage that may be done to morale and productivity.

On the other hand, some level of labour turnover is important to bring new ideas, skills and enthusiasm to the labour force.

5.4 Absenteeism

$$\text{absenteeism (\%)} = \frac{\text{number of staff absent (on a given day)}}{\text{total number of staff}} \times 100$$

Injuries and illness can be genuine causes of absenteeism. However, other more potentially damaging causes exist. Low morale, poor working conditions, inadequate training and stressful demands may all lead to employees taking time off. Absenteeism is expensive, as quality and productivity can suffer and overtime payments may be necessary for absent employees.

5.5 Health and safety

$$\text{health and safety (\%)} = \frac{\begin{array}{c}\text{number of working days lost per annum}\\\text{for health and safety reasons}\end{array}}{\text{total number of possible working days}} \times 100$$

Accidents at work can be damaging for a business in a number of ways:
- Employees may demand compensation for injuries they have suffered which, even if covered by insurance, may result in higher premiums in future years.
- The business's reputation may suffer. This may result in lower sales and greater difficulty in attracting high-calibre employees. A survey in 2000 showed that over 70% of employees would be uncomfortable working for an employer with a poor reputation.
- Production may be lost while the causes of (and solutions to) accidents are identified.

High levels of accidents may require businesses to invest in training programmes, to appoint more health and safety officers and to ensure that safe working procedures are followed at all times.

Ideas for application
The relative importance of these measures will vary according to the type of business and the market in which it operates. Thus, for example, data on health and safety might be important in high-risk industries such as oil extraction. However, productivity might be the most vital criterion in price-competitive markets such as the manufacture of small mass-produced cars.

6 Flexible workforces

Flexible workforces are those that are adaptable to changing conditions and demands. A flexible workforce is likely to be multiskilled, well-trained and not resistant to change. Performance-related pay may be used to encourage labour flexibility.

Flexible workforces can take a number of forms:
- Some of the workforce may be on part-time and temporary contracts, allowing the business to adapt smoothly to changes in the level of demand for its products.
- Employees may be on fixed short-term contracts. This is beneficial in that workers are not employed any longer than necessary and expensive redundancy payments can be avoided. However, such contracts may have a negative impact upon the motivation and performance of employees.
- Employees may work flexible hours either through flexitime or an annualised hours system. The former entails employees having to be at work during 'core hours' each day (maybe 10 a.m. until 4 p.m.) and making up the balance of hours at times that

suit them. The latter system allows employers to ask staff to work longer hours during busy periods with time taken in lieu during quieter periods.

- Employees may be required to work from a number of locations. Alternatively, they may be required to telework — to work from home, using computers and other technology to communicate with colleagues and customers.
- Multiskilled employees are an important element of a flexible workforce. Their ability to switch from one job to another as demand changes, or when colleagues are absent, allows a business to meet the demands of the market more easily and responsively.

Examiner's tip

Labour forces are an important determinant of competitiveness. Many firms have invested a lot of time, energy and training in making their employees more flexible and better able to cope with rapidly changing environments. However, there are disadvantages of flexibility, and some industries are not particularly suited to this type of labour force (e.g. those requiring low-skilled employees). This is a popular area for questions, and one on which you should relate the theory carefully to the circumstances of the question.

Advantages	Disadvantages
• Firms can more easily meet fluctuations in demand.	• Communication problems may occur if employees are used irregularly.
• It is simpler to cover for absent staff.	• Systems such as empowerment and teamworking may prove difficult to implement.
• Wage costs may be reduced.	
• Firms can meet the demand for highly specialised skills relatively cheaply.	• Lack of security may detract from employee motivation and morale.
• Firms can respond rapidly to changing circumstances.	• A higher turnover of labour may result.

Table 3.6 The advantages and disadvantages of flexible workforces

C Employer/employee relations

This relates to the atmosphere that exists within a business between the employees and their representatives (trade unions or works councils) and the employers. Communication between the two parties is a key aspect of industrial relations. Lack of effective communication can sour relations and cause disputes. In addition to communication, this term covers:

- negotiations over pay and working conditions
- employees participating in the decision-making process

1 Individual and collective bargaining

1.1 Collective bargaining

Collective bargaining is negotiation between employers and the representatives of the workforce, normally trade union officials. Collective bargaining can take place only if the employer recognises the trade union for the purposes of negotiation. A collective agreement means that all employees have to accept the outcome of the negotiation.

Collective bargaining has become less common in the UK since the 1980s. However, there is some evidence that the implementation of the Employment Relations Act in 2000 might have reversed this trend. Under this act, any trade union with a membership in excess of 50% of the employees at a place of work has the legal right to participate in collective bargaining.

1.2 Individual bargaining

Individual bargaining exists when each single employee negotiates his or her own pay and working conditions. The move to individual bargaining has accompanied the introduction of HRM into many workplaces. This assists organisations in making the most effective use of employees. They are able to encourage and reward those employees who make the most effective contribution to the business's performance. Employees who do not perform well will not benefit from collectively agreed pay settlements.

Individual bargaining is often accompanied by a strong emphasis on training and individual development to encourage employees to make the maximum possible contribution to the business.

2 *Employee participation and industrial democracy*

Industrial democracy gives employees the means of influencing the decision-making processes within a business. Most of the techniques of industrial democracy involve employee participation in the management of the business, such as worker directors.

Some businesses genuinely attempt to involve employees in decision making, while others implement relevant methods to improve public relations internally and externally.

The main methods of promoting industrial democracy and employee participation are as follows:

- **Worker directors are shop-floor representatives** who are (usually) elected to be members of the board of directors of a business. Worker directors were advocated by the Bullock Report in 1977. Unions sometimes oppose the appointment of such directors because other workers may see them as having a hand in implementing unpopular policies, so blurring the distinction between employers and employees. Managers sometimes fear that worker directors may leak sensitive financial information. In recent years the EU has encouraged the appointment of worker directors.
- **A works council** provides a basis for regular meetings between representatives from management and employees. Works councils focus on ideas to improve the performance of the organisation at all levels. Negotiations on pay and conditions are left to other forums.
- **Employee shareholder schemes** are increasingly common, giving employees shares in the company for which they work. The intention is that employees will be motivated to improve their performance by having a stake in the financial success of a business.
- **Autonomous workgroups** are delegated tasks by management and given the authority to decide how to carry out these tasks. In effect, these groups are empowered teams. The authority they are given may also extend to electing a team leader, proposing improvements in working practices and contributing to decision making. Many

businesses believe that using delegated teams is a better means of achieving industrial democracy, as it involves a large number of employees at shop-floor level.

Examiner's tip

It is important to explore the links between people and organisations and other areas of the specification, especially in synoptic papers. Clearly, some of the techniques necessary to achieve industrial democracy have considerable implications for methods of production. For example, autonomous workgroups may require a move away from a traditional production line. Exploring cross-specification links such as this can prove very fruitful.

3 Trade unions

A trade union is an organised group of employees, which aims to protect and enhance the economic position of its members.

Trade unions offer a number of **advantages to their members**:
- negotiation of pay and conditions on behalf of their members (collective bargaining)
- protection from unsafe working practices
- a range of associated services, including financial and legal advice

Employers can also benefit from the existence of trade unions for the following reasons:
- They act as a communications link between management and employees.
- Professional negotiation on behalf of a large number of employees can save time and lessen the likelihood of disputes occurring.

3.1 Types of trade union
- **General unions** comprise members with a wide range of skills, employed by firms in a variety of industries. An example is the Transport and General Workers' Union (T&G).
- **Craft unions** are the oldest type of union, whose origins lie in traditional crafts. In order to protect themselves, workers with similar craft skills formed unions. A modern example is the Musicians' Union.
- **Industrial unions** recruit members from a particular industry, such as teachers or railway workers. However, they may not represent all the employees within the particular industry. A well-known example is the National Union of Railwaymen.
- **Occupational unions** recruit from similar occupations across a range of industries. Cleaners may operate in many firms and industries but all may be members of Unison.
- **Enterprise unions** represent all employees within a particular business. They operate in cooperation with the employer, which has led to doubts being expressed about their independence. This form of unionism originated in Japan.

The distinction between the types of union has tended to blur in recent years. Traditionally, UK unionism has been a complex amalgam of the first three categories of union. This has meant that managers have had to negotiate with a number of unions over pay and conditions.

3.2 Functions of trade unions
These include at least some of the following:
- negotiating pay and working conditions (e.g. hours worked weekly or extent of holidays)

- improving job security for union members
- negotiating grievance and disciplinary procedures
- negotiating job descriptions and job specifications

Trade unions are responsible for collective bargaining in the workplace. They negotiate with employers on behalf of their members on matters such as pay, conditions and fringe benefits. Unions are in a better position to negotiate than individuals in that they have more negotiating skills and power.

Collective bargaining differs from **individual bargaining** in that the latter involves each individual employee negotiating his or her own pay and working conditions. Individual bargaining occurs when no union exists or when confident and/or talented individuals feel they will negotiate better terms on their own.

3.3 The changing role of trade unions in the UK

Union membership rose from the 1950s until the mid-1970s. Since then it has fallen steadily, though since 1999 there have been signs of a revival in union membership. This decline has occurred for a number of reasons:

- **Legislation to control the activities of unions.** The Conservative governments of the 1980s and early 1990s passed a series of acts to limit the impact of unions on business activities. In particular, this legislation made secret ballots on disputes mandatory and restricted the number of pickets.
- **The decline of traditional industries.** The shipbuilding and steel industries were strongly unionised. The fact that these industries have declined in importance and employ far fewer people means that the unions associated with them have also become less important.
- **The increasing number of small businesses.** There has been a rise in the number of small businesses in the UK since the 1980s. These firms are not strongly unionised because they employ few people (and many are part time) and relationships are such that a union is often considered unnecessary.
- There have been **significant changes in the composition of the UK's workforce** in recent years. More employees are now female and part time and less likely to be members of unions. Simultaneously, fewer young employees have entered the workforce because of falling birth rates and thus unions have had fewer potential recruits.

Other factors, apart from declining membership, have also contributed to this declining influence of unions in the UK economy:

- **Single union agreements.** These agreements have been more common since the late 1980s. Under such agreements, employees agree to be represented by one union. This makes negotiation simpler for the employers (as there are only two parties to the discussions) while reducing the possibility of disputes between rival unions. It also assists in developing single status within the organisation and eliminating differences between blue-collar and white-collar workers. And it helps maintain good communications between employers and employees, lessening the possibility of expensive and damaging industrial action.
- **No-strike deals.** This type of agreement originated in Japan and is most common among Japanese firms in the UK. While these deals have made the UK a more attractive location for international investment, they have altered the balance of power in favour of the employer. However, British unions have tended to sign them only when

binding arbitration is a part of the deal. In the event of a dispute, this means an independent third party can impose a settlement.

- **The move towards local negotiations between employers and employees.** Before the 1990s, national agreements were common in many industries. This did not necessarily reflect the situation in the local labour market or the living costs faced by employees. Equally, national settlements did not take into account the financial position of the individual business. Local negotiations have also tended to result in settlements over a longer period of time, allowing a business to plan more accurately for the future.

- **Union derecognition.** Some businesses do not recognise unions within the workplace. Although in certain cases this has been a means of achieving a single union position, in others the aim has been to eliminate unions from the workplace entirely. This process has frequently been accompanied by financial inducements to the workforce. However, the Employment Relations Act (2000) is likely to reverse this trend, as it grants unions the right to recognition as long as they have over 50 % of the workforce as members.

- **Anti-union legislation.** Throughout the 1980s, Conservative governments passed a succession of laws aimed at restricting the power of trade unions. The main acts were:
  - **Employment Act (1980).** This enabled firms to derecognise unions. It also restricted picketing to employees' 'own place of work'.
  - **Employment Act (1982).** This placed further restrictions on lawful industrial action and meant that trade unions could be sued for implementing unlawful industrial action.
  - **Trade Union Act (1984).** This made a secret ballot of employees mandatory before industrial action was lawful.
  - **Employment Act (1988).** This protected union members from being disciplined by unions for ignoring strike calls.
  - **Employment Act (1990).** This reduced the likelihood of unofficial strikes by permitting employers to dismiss workers taking this form of action. The act also effectively ended closed-shop agreements, making it illegal to refuse to employ an individual because he or she is not a member of a union.
  - **Trade Union Reform and Employment Rights Act (1993).** This required unions to provide employers with at least 7 days' notice of official industrial action. It also abolished wages councils and their imposition of minimum pay rates.

3.4 Forms of industrial action

Trade unions have a number of 'weapons' to deploy in pursuit of their aims:

- **Official strikes** occur when union members withdraw their labour with the sanction of their union, having completed the necessary legal processes, such as secret ballots. Strikes tend to be the last resort, as employees suffer a loss of wages for an indefinite period.

- **Wildcat strikes**, also termed **unofficial strikes**, may be called by either the workforce or shop stewards without the support of the union at a wider level.

- **Picketing** occurs when strikers lobby those entering workplaces where there is an industrial dispute. The intention is to prevent other workers entering the workplace. Legislation restricts the number of people able to picket at any one time.

- **Working-to-rule** involves workers following their contracts to the letter in an attempt to reduce the productivity of the workforce. Employees refuse to undertake any work that is not specified in their contract of employment.

- **Go-slows** operate when workers deliberately take longer than normal over tasks.

- **Sit-ins** take place when workers occupy their workplace with the intention of attracting the attention of the public while disrupting the normal operation of the business.

4 Settling industrial disputes

In most cases, disputes can be resolved without unions being forced into strike action. The improvement in industrial relations in recent years has, in part, been a consequence of two main techniques.

4.1 Arbitration
This can take several forms:
- **Non-binding arbitration** involves a neutral third party making an award to settle a dispute that the parties concerned can accept or not.
- **Binding arbitration** means parties to the dispute have to take the award of the arbitrator.
- **Pendulum arbitration** means the decision is binding and the arbitrator has to decide entirely for one side or the other. 'Splitting the difference' is not an option. This system avoids excessive claims by unions or miserly offers by employers.

4.2 Conciliation
Conciliation is a method of resolving individual or collective disputes in which a neutral third party encourages the continuation of negotiation rather than industrial action. The conciliator's role does not involve making any judgement concerning the validity of the position of either party.

5 Key organisations in industrial relations

A number of important institutions exist which shape the strategy and practice of industrial relations in the UK. Some of these institutions are official, acting in the interests of the government; others are independent.

5.1 Advisory, Conciliation and Arbitration Service (ACAS)
ACAS was set up in 1975 as an independent body with the responsibility to prevent or resolve industrial disputes. ACAS is financed by the government and originated during a period of severe industrial action in the 1970s when both employers and employees called for a mechanism for resolving disputes.

ACAS provides employers and employees with arbitration and conciliation services. The organisation also offers other services:
- **Advisory work.** ACAS advises employers, trade unions and employers' associations on topics such as reducing absenteeism, employee sickness and payment systems.
- ACAS **investigates individual cases** of unfair discrimination and unfair dismissal.
- Initially, ACAS was principally involved in the **resolution of industrial disputes**. More recently, the organisation has focused on **improving business practices** to reduce the possibility of industrial disputes.

5.2 Industrial tribunals
Industrial tribunals are informal 'labour courts' established to decide whether individuals have been treated unlawfully by their employers. They were established in 1964 and are found throughout the UK.

Each tribunal is chaired by someone with legal training. Most are concerned with claims for unfair dismissal. The tribunals have lost some of their informality, as most employees are represented by solicitors or barristers nowadays.

6 Employment legislation

6.1 Individual labour law

This element of employment legislation relates to the rights and obligations of individual employees. The amount of individual labour law has increased considerably in recent years, encouraged by the growing influence of the European Union on the operation of UK businesses.

The major acts are set out below:
- **The Equal Pay Act (1970)** states that both sexes should be treated equally with regard to employment. European Union law has reinforced this legislation, in particular the 1975 Equal Pay Directive.
- **The Sex Discrimination Act (1975)** prohibits discriminatory practices in recruitment, promotion and dismissal as well as ensuring equal access to benefits and services. The Equal Opportunities Commission was established to oversee and enforce this legislation.
- **The Employment Act (1975)** sets out the rights of employees not to be unfairly dismissed. The act also established the Advisory, Conciliation and Arbitration Service (ACAS).
- **The Race Relations Act (1976)** prohibits discrimination in employment against individuals on the grounds of sex, marital status, colour, nationality or ethnic origin. The Commission for Racial Equality monitors and enforces the operation of this legislation.
- **The Employment Act (Consolidation) (1978)** provides protection against unfair dismissal of employees. The act applies to those who have been employed by a business for 2 years or more. Dismissal for membership of a trade union, pregnancy or personal dislike was deemed to be unfair. The act also confirmed regulations concerning contracts of employment.
- **The Disability Discrimination Act (1995)** makes it unlawful for an employer to treat a disabled person less favourably than others without just cause. The act also requires employers to make reasonable adjustments to the working environment to assist those employees with disabilities.
- **Working Time Regulations (1998).** This European Union legislation limits the amount that employees can be required to work each week to 48 hours. Employees can choose to work longer hours, but employers cannot insist that they do so without inserting an appropriate clause in their contract of employment.
- **Minimum Wage Act (1999).** This established minimum hourly rates of pay for all employees aged over 18. These rates are updated regularly.

Examiner's tip
It is much more important to understand the implications of legislation for the behaviour of businesses than the details of the acts themselves. It is also vital to appreciate the likely responses of businesses to legislation and to be aware of new acts passed during your programme of study.

6.2 Collective labour law

These laws apply to the operation of industrial relations and collective bargaining as well as to the activities of trade unions. Industrial relations have been increasingly influenced by legislation, particularly under Conservative governments during the 1980s. The major acts applying to collective labour law were considered earlier in this section under 'Anti-union legislation' on page 111.

6.3 The impact of employment legislation

- The Conservative administrations of the 1980s and early 1990s were committed to reducing the burden of employment legislation borne by businesses. However, this intention was offset by the increasing impact of EU legislation on UK businesses. Recent EU directives have covered racial and sexual discrimination, and the free movement of employees throughout the European Union.
- Employment protection legislation results in additional costs on employers: for example, the requirement for reasonable changes to the working environment in order to encourage the employment of those with disabilities.
- Employment legislation can require firms to employ more non-productive personnel to ensure that they meet all relevant legislative requirements. For this reason, most major employers employ human relations specialists.
- Employment protection can provide the workforce with a safer and more secure working environment. Freedom from arbitrary dismissal and similar measures may encourage a more cooperative, flexible and productive workforce, enhancing the performance of the business.
- Legislation designed to improve the operation of the labour market has encouraged greater flexibility in employment: for example, the employment of temporary and part-time staff. This has helped to reduce unemployment while at the same time increasing the competitiveness of UK businesses.

This chapter covers the factors that influence location decisions, both nationally and internationally, the types and scale of production as well as modern and traditional methods of controlling production operations. Considerable emphasis is given to productive efficiency, competitiveness and the Japanese approach to production.

AS Operations management

The AS specification on operations management covers three topics: productive efficiency, controlling operations and lean production. The AS specifications for AQA, Edexcel and OCR are very similar.

A Productive efficiency

Productive efficiency means that a firm produces its output using the minimum amount of resources (e.g. labour, materials and machinery) possible. A productively efficient business is a competitive business. It can use its efficiency to reduce prices — or to enjoy enhanced profits.

Businesses can enhance their productive efficiency by:
● producing at the 'right' scale — large enough, but not too large
● using all of its resources (its capacity) as fully as possible
● adopting the most appropriate method of production

This section will consider all these influences.

1 The scale of the operation

1.1 Measuring the size of firms

There are a number of ways in which the size of firms can be measured. These include:
● number of employees
● turnover
● level of profit
● value of assets
● share of market held

The size of the business relative to other firms in the same industry can be an important determinant of performance. Scale can be critical in determining the success of a firm, since unit costs can be reduced at larger levels of output.

In general, firms are getting larger. However, there is some evidence that this trend may have peaked. In 1970, the UK's largest 100 firms produced 40% of UK output; the comparative figures for 1993 and 1996 were 35% and 33% respectively.

Firms can grow in a number of ways, as illustrated in Figure 4.1.

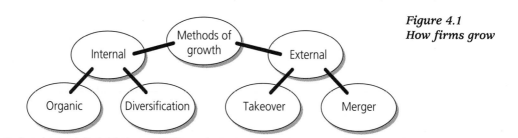

*Figure 4.1
How firms grow*

Organic growth means that the firm expands by selling more of its current products. This can be achieved by:

- outperforming competitors in existing markets (perhaps through new product development)
- selling to new markets (e.g. overseas)

This is likely to take considerable time and lack of finance might be a significant problem.

Diversification means that a firm grows by adding to its product range. A classic example of growth by diversification is Richard Branson's Virgin group.

An alternative is **external growth** by takeover or merger. A **takeover** occurs when one company purchases control of another. An example is the takeover of the National Westminster Bank by the Royal Bank of Scotland. A **merger** occurs when two or more firms agree to join together to create a single new business. In 2002 two computer manufacturers, Compaq and Hewlett Packard, merged to form a larger company with the prospect of benefiting from economies of scale.

1.2 Economies and diseconomies of scale

As firms grow in size, they begin to enjoy the benefits of **economies of scale. This means that unit production costs fall and, up to a point, efficiency and profits improve**. This offers businesses huge competitive advantages. Figure 4.2 illustrates this point.

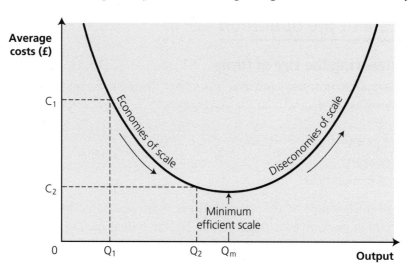

Figure 4.2 Economies and diseconomies of scale and minimum efficient scale

A firm that can only produce an output of OQ_1 will face a cost per unit of OC_1 and will have to set prices at this level (at least) or face a loss.

A larger firm producing OQ_2 will be able to price around OC_2 and, depending on price elasticity of demand, may dominate the market.

If the firm's output exceeds the minimum efficient scale (OQ_m), it will face higher unit costs if it increases its scale of output.

One reason why unit costs fall as output expands is that fixed costs are spread over more units of output.

Economies of scale can be split into two types: **internal** and **external**.

1.2a Internal economies of scale
Internal economies of scale are those factors that reduce average costs in an individual firm as it increases the scale of its operations. Examples include the following:

- **Purchasing economies**, which exist when firms are able to buy components and materials more cheaply, taking advantage of bulk discounts. They may also employ trained buyers who can negotiate the best deals.
- **Production economies**, which arise from the use of mass production techniques to speed up production. Firms producing greater quantities can afford to buy large, specialised, technically advanced machinery to lower production costs.
- **Risk-bearing economies**, which mean that larger businesses can afford to take risks when launching new products and even sustain losses to a limited degree. Such businesses can also operate an R&D department.
- **Financial economies**, which offer significant advantages to larger enterprises. Such firms are able to borrow more easily and at more favourable rates of interest, as they have greater reserves. Financial specialists may also be able to advise them on how to reduce costs further.
- **Marketing economies**, which reduce unit costs because firms can afford to advertise extensively — the extra cost is small when spread over many units of output.
- **Administrative economies**, which arise because large businesses can hire specialists to help minimise costs. Large firms can also pay high salaries and recruit the best managers.

1.2b External economies of scale
External economies of scale are the advantages of scale that benefit the whole industry and not just individual firms. So, if an industry is concentrated in one geographical area, the following benefits might be available to all the firms:

- a network of suitable and established suppliers
- a pool of skilled labour
- training courses arranged at local colleges
- a suitable infrastructure — roads, rail links, etc.

Large firms can suffer from **diseconomies of scale**. Once they are past their minimum efficient scale, the cost per unit of production begins to increase. This may be due to:

- **Over-use of existing machinery.** This increases maintenance costs and causes breakdowns.
- **Communication problems.** As the business grows, people may not know whom to report to. Managers may begin to rely on sending memos rather than speaking to people directly.
- **Marketing problems.** Managers may not concentrate on the right products.

The fact that large businesses are not necessarily more profitable than small or medium-sized businesses is evidence that diseconomies of scale do operate in the real world. The optimum size of a business may also change over time as the market, personnel and technology change.

Examiner's tip
It is often argued that economies of scale are technical in origin while diseconomies arise from problems with people (e.g. communications). There is potential for a powerful line of analysis in this distinction.

Ideas for application
Some businesses can benefit more from economies of scale than others. Firms with heavy fixed costs need to produce on a large scale to spread these fixed costs over a large number of units of output and to reduce average costs to a minimum. Similarly, economies of scale are important to businesses in fiercely price-competitive markets. This is a major reason behind the mergers that have taken place between supermarkets.

2 Production and value added

Production involves the utilisation of resources to fulfil consumers' needs. Typically, people think of manufacturing when using the term 'production', but it applies equally to service industries.

Production aims to create value added. This is the difference between the value of a business's output and the cost of the necessary inputs. Value added focuses attention on the value that a business adds to its bought-in services, components and materials through its efforts in terms of production and marketing.

Work-study is one technique aiming to make the best possible use of material and human resources in production. This technique is based on the work of **F. W. Taylor** and is often called **time and motion study**. Work-study encompasses **method study**, which analyses the way in which jobs are completed, and **work measurement**, which measures and records the time required to complete activities.

3 Types of production

Production can be classified as follows:
- **Job production** — producing a one-off item specifically designed to meet the needs of a particular customer. This type of production is commonly used when volumes of output are low and orders intermittent.
- **Batch production** — the manufacture of a limited number of identical products. Each batch of products passes through the stages of the production process together. This method offers some economies of scale when compared with job production.
- **Flow production** — the manufacture of a product through the use of a production line and a conveyor belt. This means that production time is minimised, so enhancing competitiveness. A flow system of production requires high utilisation of capacity, as

costs of production are high. Because of this, sustained demand is essential to justify the high levels of capital expenditure.

A further classification of production in the economy is as follows:

- **Primary production** — recovering and developing the world's natural resources. Examples include agriculture, forestry, fishing and mining. Employment and output in the primary sector declined significantly throughout the twentieth century.
- **Secondary production** — essentially manufacturing, or converting and processing components and raw materials. The motor vehicle industry and food processing are in the secondary sector.
- **Tertiary production** — all service industries, such as banking, retailing, health and education. This element of the UK economy has grown rapidly over recent years.

4 Constraints on production

All businesses engaged in production face a number of constraints. These vary according to the nature and scale of production, but include being subject to various legislative acts and constraints on disposing of waste.

4.1 Legislation

All firms come within the jurisdiction of acts including:
- the Health and Safety Act (1974)
- the Environmental Protection Act (1991)
- the Food Safety Act (1990)

4.2 Waste disposal

Firms, particularly in manufacturing, face considerable constraints in disposing of waste materials and products in a safe and non-polluting manner. This can increase costs of production by requiring different methods of production or more expensive methods of disposal. Recent EU legislation has tightened up rules on the disposal of many products, including oils and waste metals.

5 Productivity versus flexibility

Firms face a fundamental choice in selecting a production system. The objective of minimising costs to maintain competitiveness is more achievable if the production system produces a large volume of similar products. This might be achieved through a simple flow system. This approach allows businesses to sell their products at the lowest possible price, and might be an optimal system in a market where demand is price elastic. For example, a manufacturer of basic foodstuffs such as tinned vegetables might seek to minimise price through producing large volumes of identical products.

On the other hand, meeting customers' needs is not merely a matter of minimising costs and prices. Henry Ford's dictum that customers 'can have any colour, so long as it is black' is outdated. Customers appreciate choice and this can be the basis of differentiation. To meet the diverse needs of consumers as fully as possible, producers may need to operate a 'pull' system of production, whereby consumers' orders are fulfilled as they are placed. Such flexible production is likely to be a less cost-effective system, but can allow more freedom in pricing decisions.

6 Capacity and capacity utilisation

6.1 What is capacity?

A firm's capacity is the maximum amount that the firm is physically capable of producing if it uses its available resources to their fullest extent. Over time, a firm is likely to adjust its capacity to meet the demands of the marketplace. The following factors may affect the amount of capacity a business requires:

- the entry (or departure) of a competitor to (or from) the market
- a change in tastes or fashions, meaning higher or lower demand for the product
- new developments in products or new production techniques

A firm may adjust capacity by:

- investing in a completely new factory or office
- extending an existing facility
- closing down a factory or office permanently
- closing down a factory or office temporarily ('mothballing')

Examiner's tip

To be able to write analytically in this area, as in many others, you should appreciate the circumstances in which each of the above techniques might be employed. For example, a firm producing income elastic products may mothball a factory during a slump.

6.2 What is capacity utilisation?

Capacity utilisation measures the amount or proportion of a business's currently available capacity that is being used in production. Changes in demand and competitors' actions will affect the extent of capacity utilisation.

$$\text{capacity utilisation (\%)} = \frac{\text{current output per month}}{\text{maximum output per month}} \times 100$$

If a business under-utilises its capacity, it is said to have spare capacity. There are a number of consequences, most of which are unfavourable:

- The business is likely to face higher unit costs, as fixed overheads are spread over fewer units of output.
- This will adversely affect profits or competitiveness, since the firm is likely to charge higher prices as a consequence of excess capacity.
- Labour and other resources may be idle, which can have a negative effect on levels of motivation.
- The firm might produce more output than it can sell, leading to increased storage costs and the possibility of being forced to sell products at a discount later.
- It may be necessary to lay off staff, adversely affecting the corporate image of the business.

Because of these factors, businesses are keen to implement **strategies to avoid having spare or unutilised capacity**. There are two broad options open to the firm:

- **Increase sales to use up the available capacity.** Entering new markets might achieve this — perhaps overseas, or by finding new uses for an existing product. Kellogg's increased sales of its cornflakes by promoting them as a product to be consumed at any time of the day, not solely at breakfast.

- **Reduce the capacity available to the firm.** This is known as **rationalisation**. It may mean selling land and buildings, as well as other fixed assets, and making staff redundant. This can be a very unattractive and expensive option, and firms may lease out spare capacity, transferring employees to other jobs if possible.

Examiner's tip
Be clear about the benefits of high capacity utilisation and the methods of eliminating spare capacity. Many questions will require you to apply this knowledge to particular circumstances, so you should be prepared to apply your knowledge selectively.

A business might face circumstances in which it has **insufficient capacity** and cannot meet demand for its products. In such a situation it has two options:
- **Increase capacity** by purchasing more fixed assets (factories, machinery). This is likely to be expensive and take time to put into practice.
- **Subcontract production** by finding a supplier to manufacture part or all of the product. This is cheaper than increasing capacity and may be put into operation in the short term.

The decision depends upon whether the firm believes that the increase in demand will last. If so, it is more likely to increase its productive capacity permanently.

B Controlling operations

1 Stock control

1.1 Definition

A firm's stock can include:
- raw materials, components and work-in-progress (products being manufactured)
- finished goods to ensure that consumer demand can be satisfied
- tools and spare parts for the maintenance of essential machinery and equipment

Stock control refers to the techniques and procedures necessary to ensure that stock is ordered, delivered and handled efficiently. Effective stock control requires:
- stock rotation
- a stock re-ordering system to ensure supplies are continuously available

1.2 The costs of holding stock

Those responsible for managing a business's finances like to see stock at a minimum level because of the **high costs associated with holding stock**, which may include the following:
- There is a considerable opportunity cost. If a business has an average stockholding of £200,000 and a return on capital figure of 20%, the business could be forgoing £40,000 of income (£200,000 × 0.20) through having high stock levels.
- Storage, lighting and insurance costs will be incurred. These costs can be considerable — high-value stock may need secure buildings.
- Large areas of the factory may be used to hold stock. This space could be used to improve working conditions or production levels, so making a positive contribution to profits.

- Acquisition and order costs will be incurred, including administrative and transport costs.

On the other hand, there are **costs of not holding enough stock**. These are reduced steadily as a business holds larger quantities of stock.

- The business may run out of raw materials, resulting in downtime and idle operators and machinery.
- The business may be unable to cope with an unexpected increase in demand and customers may be lost as a result.
- Delayed deliveries may result in the loss of customers and the payment of penalties for late supply as well as damaging the firm's reputation.
- Low stock levels can lead to the need for regular, small orders, eliminating any benefits arising from purchasing in bulk.

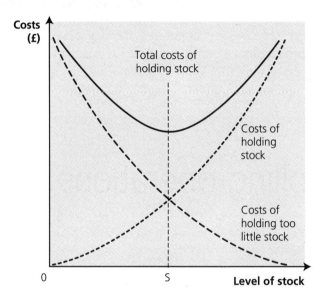

Figure 4.3 shows that, as the level of stock held by the firm increases, the costs associated with having insufficient stock fall and the costs of holding stock increase. When added together, these costs provide a U-shaped cost curve for holding stock. Firms aim to hold enough stock to minimise these total costs. In this case, they should hold stock equal to OS.

1.3 Other factors

Besides the costs of holding stocks, a number of other factors will influence businesses when taking decisions on the quantity of stock to maintain:

- **The pattern of demand.** Fluctuations in demand mean that firms may have to stockpile goods to meet sudden surges in demand. These surges may be difficult to anticipate or, as in the case of firework manufacturers, part of an annual pattern.
- **The financial position of the firm.** If a business has limited working capital, it may be forced to hold tiny quantities of stock and to re-order very small quantities frequently.
- **The type of goods produced.** Manufacturers of perishable goods may have to hold limited stock levels to avoid incurring high wastage costs.
- **Reliability of suppliers.** If supplies are certain, firms may be content to hold minimal levels of stock, as the risk of being unable to obtain further supplies is low. Alternatively, if, say, bad weather or war might interfere with supplies, larger quantities of stock might be held.

1.4 Policies for holding stock

When planning holdings of stock, firms need to consider two key factors:
- the order quantity — how much to order on each occasion
- the re-order level — how frequently to order stock

1.4a Economic order quantity (EOQ)

To calculate the economic order quantity, it is necessary to compare the delivery costs with the cost of holding stock. The result is the **optimum stock order level**. When delivery costs are high, but the costs of holding stock are low, deliveries of stock should be large and infrequent. The EOQ can be calculated by using the formula:

$$EOQ = \sqrt{\frac{2PD}{C}}$$

where P = acquisition cost, D = annual demand, C = cost of storing one unit of stock

The economic order quantity is that quantity where the cost of holding stock is equal to the cost of raising and holding an order.

The weaknesses of EOQ as a model of stock control are:
- **It ignores the buffer stock level** — that is, the minimum amount of stock the firm should hold.
- **It makes no allowance for running out of stock** — lost orders and damaged reputation.

1.4b The re-order level

The re-order level is the minimum quantity of stock a firm will hold before placing a further order with its supplier. It may be influenced by the following factors:
- the level of demand for the product and the rate at which stock is used
- the interval between the placing of the order and the arrival of stock
- the level of buffer stock held by the firm

1.5 A model of holding stock

Figure 4.4 shows perfect management of stock. The business is using its stock at a constant rate and the lead time is unchanging. Both these elements are unrealistic, but the figure does illustrate all the key features of effective stock control:
- **The economic order quantity** — the difference between the minimum and the maximum stock levels. This helps to keep stockholding costs to a minimum.
- **The minimum stock level** — an amount of stock designed to protect against surges in demand or delays in supply.

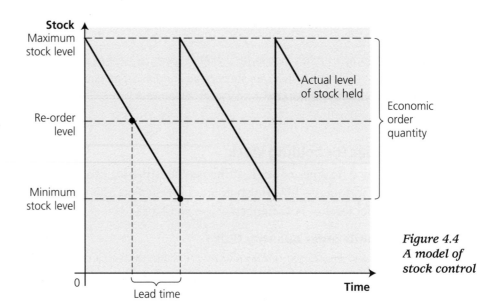

*Figure 4.4
A model of
stock control*

- **The maximum stock level** — the minimum level plus the EOQ. Holding more than this level of stock means the firm will incur heavy stockholding costs.
- **The re-order level** — the amount of stock that acts as a trigger to place an order for further stock from suppliers.
- **The lead time** — the gap between placing an order and the arrival of the stock.

Managing stock in this manner is sometimes referred to as a **just-in-case** system.

1.6 Recent developments in stock control

1.6a Computerised stock control

Businesses frequently hold details of their entire stock on a database. All additions to and uses of stock can be immediately recorded and up-to-date stock levels can be found instantly and detailed on a stock printout.

1.6b Automatic re-ordering of stock

Some stock control systems are automatically programmed to re-order stock at the re-order level. Through use of the bar code system, supermarkets monitor sales of stock and each sale is subtracted from the total stock level held.

1.6c Just-in-time stock control

This is part of a production system intended to minimise the costs of holding stocks of raw materials, components and finished goods. JIT schedules deliveries to arrive at the next stage of production (or customers) just at the time they are required. As a consequence, businesses can operate with minimal stock levels. This technique is a part of the so-called **Japanese approach**. This is considered more fully later in this chapter (pages 128–129).

Ideas for application

Stock is a very important issue for certain businesses. The costs of holding stock are likely to be high for a jeweller because of security and the value of the items themselves. It is a matter of importance to a baker because of the perishable nature of the products. Try to consider if and why holding stock might be an important issue to the business in any examination scenario.

2 *Quality control and quality assurance*

A quality product is one that meets customers' needs fully. Quality is a major determinant of a business's competitiveness and has attracted a great deal of attention over recent years.

If a firm produces poor-quality products, it incurs:
- the costs of scrapping or reworking products
- additional costs if customers return goods for repair under warranty
- costs (which are more difficult to measure) associated with damage to the reputation of the business

2.1 Quality control

There is an important distinction between quality control and quality assurance. **Quality control is the process of checking that completed production meets agreed criteria.** Quality control inspectors usually undertake this task, though some factories encourage employees to check their own quality. However, quality control only identifies problems once the production process is complete. Quality control also aims to improve product design and entails the regular review of quality control procedures.

2.2 Quality assurance

Quality assurance is implemented to ensure that quality standards are attained by all employees in a business. The aim is to maximise customer satisfaction and hence sales and profits. This policy affects all activities in the organisation and is intended to prevent problems, such as defective products, from occurring in the first place.

There are two main **quality assurance systems** in operation: total quality management and BSI quality assurance.

2.2a Total quality management

Total quality management (TQM) instils a culture of quality throughout the organisation. TQM places on all employees of a firm an individual and collective responsibility for maintaining high quality standards. It aims for prevention rather than detection, with a target of zero defects (see Figure 4.5).

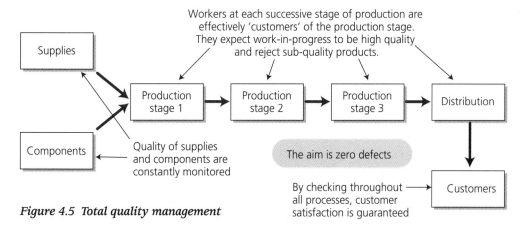

Figure 4.5 Total quality management

TQM originated in Japan and was based on the work of an American consultant, Edward Deming. In the 1950s and 1960s, Japanese products were regarded as relatively cheap but inferior versions of products manufactured in western economies. In response to this,

Japanese companies began to develop the philosophies and systems necessary to acquire a reputation for quality products.

TQM has both an internal and an external dimension. Externally, the success of a firm depends upon its ability to satisfy the demands of its external customers. Product quality is likely to be a way in which a company can achieve a competitive advantage. Internally, each department in a firm is viewed as a customer and/or a supplier. The firm has to meet high standards in this 'internal' trading — the flow of raw materials, components and finished goods through to the dispatch department.

Quality assurance systems are unlikely to succeed without the support of the whole workforce. Workers must understand and comply with them. TQM seeks to establish a unity of interest and commitment to the maintenance of the highest possible quality standards in each of the internal transactions. It seeks to minimise the amount of time and money spent on quality control by preventing quality problems. Individual commitment to quality can be reinforced by the operation of quality circles (see page 84) and other employee participation schemes.

TQM ensures that products are constantly monitored throughout manufacture. Workers at each stage of the process examine critically the work-in-progress they receive. Errors and faults are identified and rectified at the earliest possible stage, and customer satisfaction is assured.

2.2b Quality assurance to ISO 9000

This is a standard operated jointly by the British Standards Institute (BSI) and the International Standards Organisation (ISO). Businesses have to meet criteria to receive certification that this standard is being met. They have to establish and maintain an effective quality system to demonstrate that products or services conform to it.

BSI and ISO systems are based on documentary evidence that specified procedures and processes are followed. Hence, they can become very bureaucratic. As a result, critics have said that this quality system says more about the firm's adherence to procedures than about the actual quality of their products or services.

In spite of this criticism, ISO 9000 remains an important international indicator of quality and some firms will not trade with businesses that are not certified.

Ideas for application

Quality has become a more important issue during the past 20 years. For some businesses it is an alternative to competing in terms of price. It is very important for any service industry, but also for firms producing high-quality and high-technology products such as laptop computers.

3 *Value analysis or value engineering*

This is the review of the design of a product. **Value analysis aims to reduce the costs of production without reducing the quality or performance of the product in question.** It may be possible to identify cheaper materials or components, or more cost-effective production processes.

An important aspect of value analysis is to ensure that the process does not diminish consumer satisfaction, although some businesses have used the technique as a means to

cut costs irrespective of quality. Market research may be necessary to assess the reactions of consumers to proposed changes.

C Lean production

The concept of **lean production** is increasingly used to describe the organisational goals of manufacturing industry. Sometimes called the **Japanese approach**, this term describes a range of measures designed to use fewer inputs and resources. The measures include:

- cell production
- just-in-time production
- kaizen or continuous improvement
- benchmarking against market leaders
- time-based management and simultaneous engineering

1 Lean production and mass production

Some managers contend that lean production has replaced mass production as the world's most efficient system of manufacturing.

Mass production is characterised by:

- standard products with little variety
- time-consuming changeovers
- infrequent new products
- the need to avoid disruption by holding buffer stocks

World-class manufacturers believe that such an approach is outdated. Customers today want new and varied products quickly. But they also want to see product quality and product performance increase without an increase in price.

World-class factories of the future will be lean producers, characterised by:

- teams of multiskilled workers
- highly flexible machinery
- lower volumes in greater variety
- very high responsiveness
- a commitment to total quality

Lean production requires less of everything:

- less human effort in the factory
- less manufacturing space
- less investment in capital
- fewer hours to develop new products
- a reduction in changeover times from hours to minutes

Table 4.1 compares the main features of mass production and lean production.

Mass production	Lean production
Unskilled jobs and employees	Highly skilled employees
Mindless workers	Motivated workers
Inflexible equipment	Flexible equipment
Identical parts in bulk	High variety

Table 4.1
Mass production
versus lean
production

2   *The techniques of lean production*

2.1 Cell production

Cell production divides the activities on the production line into a series of independent units. Each of these units, known as **cells**, is self-contained. The idea, which originated in the Soviet Union, is intended to improve quality and motivation. Each cell should have a team leader supported by a number of multiskilled staff.

Quality is likely to be improved because later cells can become the customers of earlier cells and will reject any substandard items. This imposes a regular and rigorous check on quality and reduces the chance of customers receiving poor-quality products.

Motivation can also be enhanced because employees are given the authority to check their own work to ensure quality. In addition, working in a cell means that employees are involved in producing a complete product (even if it is only a component). Seeing an outcome of their efforts can stimulate workers to improve their performance.

Cell production usually operates alongside the just-in-time approach to production.

2.2 Just-in-time manufacturing

Just-in-time (JIT) manufacturing is a Japanese management philosophy that involves having the right items of the right quality in the right place at the right time. JIT is a central component of lean production.

2.2a The origins of JIT

The initial ideas originated in Japanese shipyards in an attempt to reduce the huge sums of money tied up in raw materials. JIT was developed and perfected in the Toyota factories by Taiichi Ohno as a means of meeting consumer demands with minimal costs and delays. Taiichi Ohno is often called the 'father' of JIT.

In the 1960s, Toyota worked hard on developing a whole range of new approaches to manufacturing. The oil crisis of the early 1970s accelerated this process and other Japanese manufacturers copied them. In Japan, work takes precedence over leisure — it is common for people to work 14-hour days. This cultural feature not only encouraged the development of JIT, but also helped to ensure its subsequent success.

2.2b The philosophy of JIT

Just-in-time manufacturing is not one technique or even a set of techniques, but an overall philosophy embracing both old and new techniques. The philosophy is based on **eliminating waste**. Waste means anything other than the minimum level of equipment, materials, parts, space and workers' time. Thus JIT means using the minimum amount of resources to satisfy customer demand.

2.2c Value added and non-value added activities

To comprehend JIT fully, it is important to distinguish between value added and non-value added activities within the business:

- **Value added activities** are those that actually convert the raw materials and components as part of the manufacturing process. These activities occur on the production line.
- **Non-value added activities** are those where the raw materials, components or finished products are not being worked upon. Examples include storage and repairing faulty products.

Japanese firms employing JIT focus upon reducing the time spent on non-value added activities, thus eliminating waste. Traditional UK management has concentrated upon making value added activities more productive through methods such as work-study. In a typical UK factory, a product spends 95% of its time in non-value added activities. At these times the product earns nothing yet still incurs costs.

It is usual to measure the level of waste in an organisation by measuring stock levels. High stock levels tend to hide quality problems, scrap, machine down-times and late deliveries. JIT is designed to highlight such issues.

2.2d Key characteristics of JIT

- It allows an organisation to meet consumer demand at whatever level it exists. **JIT is a 'pull' system of production.**
- It is based on demand-pull production — demand signals when a product should be manufactured. Use of demand-pull enables a firm to produce only what is required in the appropriate quantity and at the correct time.
- Suppliers of components and other materials must be very responsive to orders from the manufacturer.
- It allows a reduction in raw materials, work-in-progress and finished goods inventories. This frees up a greater amount of space within factories.
- The layout of the factory is arranged for maximum worker flexibility, encouraging the use of multiskilled employees.
- It requires high levels of training to give workers the skills necessary to carry out a number of tasks.
- Employees engage in self-inspection to ensure that their products are of high quality and that value has been added.
- Continuous improvement is an integral part of JIT.

2.3 Kaizen or continuous improvement

2.3a Key points

- **Kaizen means 'continuous improvement' and is a very important element of lean production.**
- It entails continual but small advances in production techniques, each improving productivity a little. The cumulative effect of these small improvements is shown in Figure 4.6.

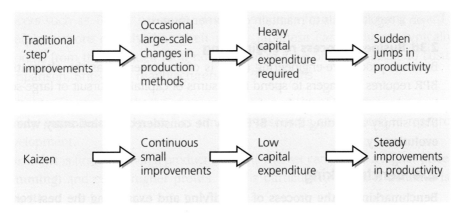

Figure 4.6 The contrast between continuous improvements under lean production and traditional 'step' improvements in productivity

- Kaizen groups meet regularly to discuss problems and to propose new ideas to improve productivity.

possible time. Some aspects of production development can be carried out at the same time, allowing products on to the market faster, cutting costs and generating revenue earlier than would otherwise have been the case.

Ideas for application

Time is an important competitive weapon in industries where products are relatively undifferentiated and the same or similar technology is available to most businesses. Thus manufacturers of vacuum cleaners strive to be the first to introduce new technology, so they can enjoy a brief period of superiority and premium pricing.

A2 Operations management

This section builds upon the material covered at AS. It is recommended that you re-read the AS materials alongside those that follow. Although A2 questions will focus on the following topics, it is likely that some of the principles covered at AS will be needed to support your answers.

A Productive efficiency

Productivity measures output of goods and services in relation to the resources (labour, raw materials) needed to produce them. Productively efficient firms use relatively small amounts of inputs to produce a unit of output. Firms seek to improve their productivity in order to reduce costs and improve their competitiveness.

1 Measuring and increasing productivity

1.1 Measuring productivity

Productivity can be measured in several ways. A common one is to measure the output of labour over some agreed time period. The following formula can be used:

$$\text{labour productivity} = \frac{\text{output (per year)}}{\text{number of employees}}$$

Increases in productivity are not simply the result of employees working harder. They may have better equipment following an investment programme. Other factors, such as training, may also help improve labour productivity.

An alternative approach is to measure capital productivity. This can be achieved by use of the following formula:

$$\text{capital productivity} = \frac{\text{output (per year)}}{\text{capital employed}}$$

Both capital and labour productivity measures do not fully assess the efficiency of an enterprise, since each considers only a single input in relation to final output. A fuller assessment would require that all inputs were considered in relation to final output.

Productivity improvements can help turn around the fortunes of a business. Gaining greater output from a given amount of inputs helps a company to reduce costs, granting it the freedom to reduce its prices, to increase its competitiveness or to take a greater profit margin.

Examiner's tip

You must look beyond the obvious when analysing data such as those relating to productivity. For example, one firm might have higher labour productivity than another. This does not necessarily mean that the firm with the higher labour productivity is more competitive. It may be that the other firm pays lower wages, enjoys favourable exchange rates or has higher capital productivity. The concept of productivity also tells us little or nothing about the quality of products.

1.2 Methods of improving productivity

- **Training.** Employees are likely to increase productivity if they have the skills necessary to carry out their jobs effectively and efficiently. If employees are multiskilled, they are more able to cover for absent colleagues or to respond to sudden increases in demand. Besides increasing skills, training can motivate employees by fulfilling social and self-esteem needs as identified by Maslow.
- **Flexible employees.** Competitive businesses need flexible workforces that can respond to the needs of consumers. Thus, part-time employees, specialists on short-term contracts and temporary employees all help a business to meet the varying demands of customers in a cost-effective manner.
- **Motivation.** Techniques to improve motivation (e.g. job enrichment and teamworking) may result in employees being more committed to the organisation and producing larger quantities of better-quality output.
- **Capital expenditure.** To maintain productivity at the levels achieved by the most efficient businesses, it is essential to provide the labour force with the tools to do the job. Car manufacturers have increased productivity significantly by investing in robotic equipment for the production line. Such equipment can be used 24 hours a day and produces consistently high-quality products.
- **Ensuring high capacity utilisation.** A business can operate most efficiently and productively through using all the capacity available to it. Greater utilisation of premises, employees and equipment contributes to lower unit costs of production and an increase in productivity as economies of scale are achieved.

2 Research and development

2.1 Definition

Research is the scientific investigation that is necessary to discover new products. It includes diverse techniques such as laboratory research and brainstorming. **Development** involves bringing the ideas with the greatest potential on to the market, thereby converting good ideas into commercial products. The intention is to satisfy customers and generate handsome profits, though this can take considerable time.

Research and development (R&D) takes place before a product is launched — that is, before the commencement of the product life cycle. This may result in the business facing difficulties with its cash flow. However, a successful business may be able to subsidise new products from more established ones (cash cows).

However, when a product enters the growth and maturity stages of the life cycle, it might be appropriate to invest in new R&D for the next generation of products. This may need to occur even earlier if the new products are likely to take time to develop. In the case of some pharmaceutical products, it can take up to 20 years to turn an idea into a commercial product.

2.2 Benefits of research and development

- Businesses can gain **a significant competitive advantage** by being the first to bring a new product on to the market. Sony achieved high sales and profits when it introduced the first personal stereo. A high-technology product with no direct rivals allows firms to charge high prices (**price skimming**).
- Businesses can gain **a reputation for producing high-quality and sophisticated products**. This image can boost sales of other, related products.
- **Patents** can be used to protect business ideas for a period of up to 20 years, allowing inventors to generate substantial earnings from their research and innovation. Many companies (e.g. Guinness) allow other businesses to produce their products in other parts of the world under licence.

2.3 Disadvantages of research and development

- Research can be **very expensive** and only large firms can afford to engage in it. Pharmaceutical firms spend millions of pounds developing new products and most of their ideas fail. About one in a hundred ideas actually makes it on to the market.
- The **time-scale can be lengthy**, meaning investors have to wait a long time for a return on their money. This may not be viable unless the business has other profitable products on the market at the same time.
- Other companies may adopt **'me too' products** that are similar (but not too similar) to the product resulting from the expensive research. These 'me too' products will enjoy some of the sales associated with the original product. Filofax, for example, took some time to develop, but imitations soon posed direct competition.
- To succeed in highly competitive markets, firms must **continuously research and sell new products**. It is not enough to have a single successful product, since at some point sales will decline as newer, more advanced products enter the market.

Examiner's tip

Questions requiring evaluative responses can be set on topics such as research and development. High-quality answers would recognise that there are two sides to the argument about whether firms should invest large sums in R&D. This provides the basis for evaluation. The decision might depend upon the actions of competitors, the finance available to the company and so on.

2.4 Protecting intellectual property

Once businesses have spent enormous sums on innovating new products, they wish to protect their investments. Governments offer **legal protection** in such circumstances to encourage research and development and competitive businesses.

- **Patents** provide protection for products and processes for a period of up to 20 years. A new processor for computers might have a patent on it.
- **Copyrights** provide protection for the creators and owners of legal documents. They can last for up to 70 years after the death of the author and are granted automatically. They apply to books, music and cartoons.
- **Trademarks** grant legal ownership of recognisable signs and symbols for an indefinite period. Firms such as Adidas use trademarks to protect their symbols, and Perrier prevents rivals copying the shape and colour of the bottles in which it sells mineral water. The 1994 Trade Marks Act brought UK legislation in this area into line with the EU.

Ideas for application

R&D is vital in industries such as pharmaceuticals which spend enormous sums of money on developing new products. The same is true of any technologically based industry, including computer hardware and software as well as the growing biotechnology industries.

B Locating the enterprise

Most businesses seek to minimise costs when taking location decisions. To do otherwise would mean that competitiveness would be hindered and profits diminished. Increasingly, location decisions have an international dimension as companies seek to trade throughout world markets.

1 The factors influencing location

1.1 Power and raw materials

- **Primary industry**, such as mining and other extractive industries, has to be located near to raw materials. Deposits of raw materials such as coal, iron ore and oil determine the location of this industry. Such 'traditional' factors are of limited importance in modern location decisions. Gas and electricity are available in almost all parts of the UK, and modern transport systems now carry goods cheaply and efficiently throughout the country.
- According to **Weber's Law**, bulk-reducing firms will locate near to their source of raw materials, since it is more expensive to transport the raw materials than the finished product.

1.2 Markets

- The location of many firms is determined by their need to be close to their markets. According to Weber's Law, businesses which produce goods that are more bulky than the raw materials used to make them are likely to locate close to their markets. The components and materials used to brew beer, for example, are far less bulky than the final product because of the water that is added during the brewing process.
- Suppliers of components and intermediate goods may set up close to their major customers.

1.3 Labour

- Firms relocating may take most of their existing staff with them. This helps to reduce disruption and the expense of recruiting new staff.
- There are shortages of particular skills among the labour force in certain areas of the UK. Some regions have labour forces that possess certain skills. For example, a firm considering food processing might find Norfolk attractive because a suitably trained labour force already exists there. Where an industry is already concentrated in a particular region, advantages are often available, such as research facilities in nearby universities and established suppliers of components. These benefits are known as **external economies of scale**.

1.4 Site

- Firms seek **different sites** when relocating — a factory unit on a modern industrial estate, an old factory in need of modernisation or a renovated warehouse offering retail possibilities. Firms will consider the cost relative to other sites, the amount of space available and the potential for expansion. Overall, firms seek sites with suitable facilities at the lowest possible cost. Investment appraisal techniques may be used to take such decisions.
- Businesses will also seek **good infrastructure** — transport and communication links are important. Many modern businesses locate near to motorways.
- **Greenfield sites** are popular and are suitable for high-tech industries. Such sites are usually on the outskirts of towns and cities, and have not been built on before. It is often cheaper and easier to build on them. However, the use of greenfield sites frequently attracts opposition from environmental pressure groups, which may damage a firm's image.

1.5 Government influence

- The government influenced the location of businesses through the operation of a **regional policy** for most of the twentieth century. The intention was to raise incomes in poor regions in the UK and to promote economic prosperity and employment throughout the country. It attempted to persuade businesses to move to areas such as South Wales and the north of England, which had seen prosperity decline along with the old 'staple' industries such as coal, shipbuilding and textiles. During the 1980s, the government reduced its role in the economy and this was reflected in a scaling down of regional policy. Relatively few areas now receive government aid to attract businesses.
- The government offers considerable assistance to firms locating in very specific areas. **Regional Selective Assistance** (RSA), for example, is paid in instalments to firms that create employment in designated areas of the UK. They can claim for expenditure on land, buildings, plant and machinery.
- **Local authority assistance** might include grants, loans or guarantees for borrowing. Local authorities may also invest directly in the business.
- **The Single Regeneration Budget**, financed by the European Union, provides support for regenerating depressed areas to allow economic development and promote competitiveness. Bids are required before funding is given. In recent years a requirement has been that any proposals must be demonstrated to be environmentally friendly.
- **Enterprise areas**, announced in the Budget of 2002, are small, deprived, inner-city areas into which the government is hoping to attract businesses by reducing

bureaucracy and offering financial incentives, such as supporting private investment with government cash.

- Firms that locate in **free zones** (small areas next to ports or airports) avoid UK customs duties. In this way, they can import raw materials and re-export at a low price due to the tax advantages. Tobacco companies often locate in free zones.

Two other major **EU sources of funds** are available:

- The **European Regional Development Fund** is aimed at reducing regional differences in terms of prosperity and assisting disadvantaged regions, particularly run-down areas facing industrial decline as well as impoverished rural areas.
- The **European Social Fund** aims to improve employment opportunities in the European Union by providing financial support towards the running costs for vocational training schemes, guidance and counselling projects as well as general job creation measures.

2 International location

Throughout the developed world, the size of firms is growing, principally through mergers. This means that an increasing number of firms have locations in more than one country. Businesses that operate (as opposed to just selling) in more than one country are known as **multinationals**.

International location operates on exactly the same principles as domestic location theory. Multinationals seek the lowest-cost location to maximise profits. Governments often offer incentives such as grants and benefits to multinationals for locating in their countries. The UK spends considerable sums of money in order to attract inward investment into the country (see Figure 4.8).

Source: Adapted from the Invest UK website: www.invest.uk.com/investor_services.

Figure 4.8 The Invest UK website

Multinationals seek the following when taking location decisions:
- effective communications systems and transport networks
- trained and productive labour available at relatively low rates of pay
- low rates of taxation levied on business profits
- local and national government grants to support the heavy investment necessary
- support services (e.g. components, R&D) readily available

In addition, they consider a number of other factors:
- **Political stability.** A firm does not want to risk any disruption of its activities.
- The need to avoid adverse **exchange rate fluctuations.** This might be an argument for locating in countries using the euro. Some Asian car manufacturers have suggested that they might move from the UK to European countries using the euro to remove the risk of adverse exchange rate fluctuations.
- **The need to avoid tariffs or other trade barriers.** One of the attractions for foreign businesses of locating in the UK is that they are able to trade within the EU's common external tariff.

Location decisions are becoming critical as more and more businesses sell their products in global markets. Taking location decisions is likely to require the application of important quantitative techniques.
- **Investment appraisal techniques.** Payback, average rate of return and discounted cash-flow techniques may assist managers in making objective choices between two or more locations. The site that offers the speediest return on the initial investment, or the greatest return over, say, a 10-year period, may be thought the most appealing.
- **Break-even analysis**. Another method of comparison may be to examine the site that requires the lowest level of output and sales to break even. This may be the chosen location.

Although quantitative techniques such as those outlined above may play an important part in the decision, ultimately the judgement is likely to be based on a mixture of qualitative and quantitative factors. This is not uncommon in business.

Ideas for application

Location is particularly important to some businesses in maintaining their competitiveness, especially if they employ large numbers of relatively unskilled workers. In 2002 famous UK manufacturers Dyson (vacuum cleaners) and Hornby (toys) took the decision to move overseas to benefit from lower wage costs. Without these moves, they argued, they would be unable to compete in terms of price with foreign businesses.

C Planning operations

Planning helps firms to decide how they will meet the requirements of customers in the most profitable manner. **Operations management** involves a great deal of planning to ensure that materials, labour and fixed assets are combined efficiently. A number of techniques, such as **Gantt charts** and **critical path analysis**, can be used to aid planning.

1 Gantt charts

A Gantt chart is a horizontal bar chart frequently used to plan production. The activities necessary to complete a project are shown in the correct sequence. Gantt charts are designed to minimise the use of resources and to coordinate the various stages of an activity. Activities are on the vertical axis and time is on the horizontal scale. Figure 4.9 is an example.

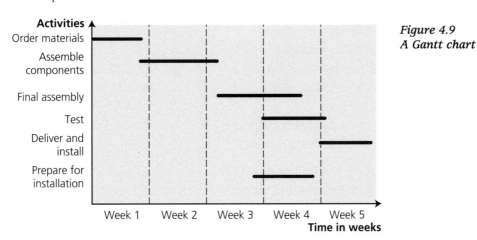

Figure 4.9
A Gantt chart

A Gantt chart allows managers to ensure that the sequence of operations is planned sensibly to minimise wasted time and to ensure that the task is completed as speedily as possible.

2 Critical path analysis

Critical path analysis (CPA) is a method of calculating and illustrating how complex projects can be completed as quickly as possible. CPA shows:
● the sequence in which the tasks must be undertaken
● the length of time taken by each task
● the earliest time at which each stage can commence

It offers substantial benefits to businesses in planning the most efficient use of their resources. This can help to minimise costs and enhance competitiveness.

A CPA **network** consists of two elements, both of which are shown in Figure 4.10.
● **Activities.** These, shown by arrows, are part of a project requiring time and probably the firm's resources. The arrows (running from left to right) show the sequence of the tasks. They are frequently given letters to denote the order. The duration of each task is written below the arrow. Some (but not all) activities cannot be started until others are concluded.
● **Nodes.** These are the start or finish of an activity and are represented by circles. Each node is numbered (in the left-hand segment) and also states the 'earliest start time' (EST) and 'latest finish time' (LFT).

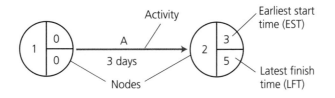

Figure 4.10
Activities and
nodes in critical
path analysis

2.1 An example of using CPA

A company is planning to increase capacity by extending its factory. The expansion is expected to cause disruption and the management team is keen to complete it as quickly as possible. The building firm has listed the major activities it will carry out as well as the expected duration of each.

Activity	Expected duration (weeks)
A Design the factory extension	6
B Obtain planning permission	4
C Dig and lay foundations	3
D Order construction materials	2
E Construct walls and roof	12
F Design interior	2
G Install production equipment	6
H Train staff in new techniques	16

The building firm has also provided the following information:
- Activity A is the start of the project.
- B starts when A is complete.
- C, D and F follow B.
- E follows C and D.
- H follows B.
- G follows F.

The network for the factory extension is shown in Figure 4.11.

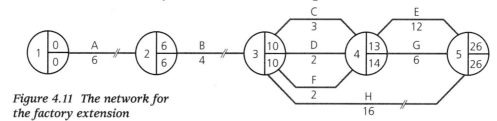

Figure 4.11 The network for the factory extension

The critical path shows the sequence of activities that must be completed on time if the whole project is not to be delayed. It is indicated by two small dashes across the relevant activities. In Figure 4.11 the critical path is A-B-H.

2.2 Earliest start times and latest finish times

The network in Figure 4.11 shows the earliest start times (ESTs) and latest finish times (LFTs) in the nodes.

2.2a Earliest start time

The EST shows the earliest time at which a particular activity can be commenced. ESTs are calculated by working from left to right and adding the times taken to complete the previous activity. If there is more than a single activity, the activity with the longest duration is included in the calculation.

The EST is recorded in the top of the two quadrants in the right-hand half of the node. The EST at node 4 is 13 days. This is because although activities D and F are complete after 12 days, activity E cannot commence until both C and D are complete. C is not complete until the end of day 13.

The EST on the final node shows the earliest date at which the whole project can be concluded.

2.2b The latest finishing time

The LFT records the time by which an activity must be completed if the entire project is not to be delayed.

LFTs are calculated from right to left. From each LFT the activity with the longest duration is deducted. The LFT at node 3 is 10 days — the 26 days from node 5 less the 16 days of activity H.

Calculating LFTs helps to highlight those activities in which there is some slack time or float.

2.3 The critical path

Those nodes in which EST = LFT (i.e. there is no float time) denote the critical path. The critical path:

- comprises those activities that take longest to complete
- allows managers to focus on those activities that must not be delayed for fear of delaying the entire project
- helps managers identify where additional resources might be needed to avoid any possibility of overrunning on projects

2.4 Float time

Float time is spare time that exists within a project. Thus, if an activity that takes 5 days has an allowance of 7 days in a network, 2 days of float time exist. In Figure 4.11, if activity E were delayed by 1 day, there would be no impact upon the entire project.

There are two types of float: **total float** and **free float**.

2.4a Total float

Total float is the reserve time available for an activity. This can be used without delaying the entire project. Subtracting the duration of an activity from the LFT and then subtracting the EST gives the total float. The formula to calculate total float is:

> **LFT (current activity) – duration – EST (current activity)**

2.4b Free float

The amount of time by which an individual activity can be delayed without affecting any following activity is termed **free float**. The formula for calculating free float is:

> **EST (following activity) – duration – EST (current activity)**

2.5 The advantages and disadvantages of CPA

2.5a Advantages

- CPA encourages managers to undertake detailed planning, which helps reduce the risk of delays and other problems.
- The resources needed for each activity can be made available at the appropriate time, so reducing costs.
- Time can be saved by operating certain activities simultaneously. This can be vital in industries where time is an important competitive weapon.
- If delays and problems do occur, the network will assist in working out a solution.

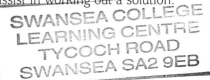

2.5b Disadvantages

- Complex activities may be impossible to represent on a network.
- The project still requires management even after the initial network is drawn, as external factors may change.
- Much depends upon how accurately the durations of activities are estimated. These can be difficult to forecast and, if they are wrong, the whole process may be of little value.

This second weakness led the US government, when developing the Polaris missile in the 1960s, to develop a system of estimating durations based on probabilities. This technique became known as **programme evaluation and review technique** (PERT).

Examiner's tip

Make sure that you concentrate on the advantages and disadvantages of key techniques such as critical path analysis. This will help you to write analytically and evaluatively when required.

Ideas for application

CPA has an important role to play in industries that have complex projects to manage, such as construction (e.g. the building of Terminal Five at Heathrow). By scheduling the use of resources effectively, CPA can reduce the amount required and help to minimise costs.

D Information technology and businesses

Information technology (IT) plays an important and rapidly developing role in business. It can assist in a number of important functions within the organisation.

- **Processing data.** Businesses collect enormous amounts of data on their customers, which can be stored in a database. When particular information is required, the database can be searched and the relevant information extracted. IT has particular application to marketing. Businesses can find out more about their customers' needs and respond directly to them. Supermarkets such as Tesco and Sainsbury use their loyalty cards to collect huge amounts of data on customers, enabling them, for example, to target special offers effectively.
- **Financial control.** Most firms store their financial records on computers and use them to produce budgets and financial statements and to operate pay systems for employees. Additionally, funds can be transferred by computer, both nationally and internationally. EFTPOS (electronic funds transfer at point-of-sale) systems, such as Switch and Delta, allow customers to pay for products without writing out cheques and without delays. Many companies also use computers to ensure strict credit control — letters are issued automatically to customers who are late with payments.
- **Electronic data interchange (EDI).** EDI is a permanent link between computers in different organisations or in different branches of the same business. This system allows the latest information to be transferred instantly from one location to another.

The information may relate to sales figures, financial data or the automatic re-ordering of supplies. Increasing numbers of businesses are using EDI.

- **Computer-aided design (CAD).** CAD uses computers to design new products and redesign existing ones using multidimensional images. This avoids the need to commence work again, as well as offering views of the design from various angles. It affords a cheap and quick means of altering designs and evaluating the options. CAD has reduced the time and cost of the design stage in production.

- **Computer-aided manufacture (CAM).** CAM utilises computers in a range of manufacturing tasks, including the use of robots in the production process. CAD and CAM systems can be linked to allow flexible specialisation, permitting businesses to meet the precise (and different) needs of each customer.

- **Manufacturing resource planning (MRPII).** This system models the entire production process. The model takes into account all the resources that are required for manufacturing, and assists managers in matching orders and available capacity. Thus, potential problems can be highlighted at the outset and appropriate action taken rather than the business failing to fulfil orders.

- **The internet.** The internet (or World Wide Web) is an electronic network used to exchange ideas and information across the globe. It has enormous commercial possibilities. Since 1995, payments have been possible on the internet through use of credit cards. This has meant that a huge range of goods and services can be bought and sold electronically, giving relatively small firms the possibility of selling worldwide. The rapid growth of the Amazon bookshop is a successful example of internet enterprise. Most businesses operate websites on the internet to promote the business and its products.

One of the key objectives of this chapter for both AS and A2 is to identify and evaluate a range of external factors that can have an enormous impact upon businesses. These factors may be economic, social, political, legal or technical, and are not always easy to predict.

It is important to appreciate that we are interested in the impact of, say, economic factors on businesses rather than the economic theory itself. It is easy to become too involved in the intricacies of, for example, fiscal or monetary policy and to lose sight of why we are studying the topic.

It is equally important to appreciate that external influences offer opportunities to businesses as well as constraining their activity. For example, while membership of the European Union may constrain the activities of UK firms due to more intense competition from European rivals, it also offers great opportunities for UK businesses in terms of new and larger markets.

The external environment is a dynamic aspect of business studies. New laws are enacted frequently by the UK government and EU authorities. Economic conditions alter (sometimes due to government actions) and technological change is ever more rapid. This dynamism makes the external environment a fascinating area to study.

AS External influences

The major topics covered at AS are markets and competition, economic influences such as inflation and unemployment, business law, social responsibilities and business ethics. The specifications for AQA, Edexcel and OCR are similar, except that the latter two leave the study of business ethics until the A2 part of the course.

A Introduction

There are a number of ways of categorising (and hopefully remembering) external influences on businesses. One useful technique is to memorise the term **SLEPT**. This stands for the following categories:

- **S**ocial
- **L**egal
- **E**conomic
- **P**olitical
- **T**echnical

SLEPT summarises the influences that you may wish to consider when answering questions on the external environment. In responding to longer and more open questions such as essays, this may also lend structure to your thinking and to your writing.

1 *Markets and competition*

A market is a place where buyers and sellers meet. The most immediate external influence faced by a business is the market within which it operates. A given market operates according to the number of firms trading within it and the degree of competition. This type of categorisation allows the likely effects on the business to be identified and analysed. The categories are outlined below.

1.1 Monopoly

A pure monopoly occurs when there is **only one supplier in a market**. Examples include the Post Office (delivering letters within the UK) and Transco (piping gas throughout the UK). A monopolistic market may exhibit some or all of the following characteristics:
- a single producer able to charge relatively high prices
- lack of innovation, which means that consumers do not receive the most up-to-date products
- inefficient use of resources

True monopolies rarely exist today, particularly since the implementation of the single European market. UK monopolies are open to competition from foreign rivals, especially those from within the European Union. Monopolies can exploit consumers and may make inefficient use of resources, so they are subject to strict controls by the UK government and the European Union (for more on this, see page 157).

1.2 Oligopoly

A market is said to be oligopolistic when **few enough firms exist for them to be inter-dependent in their actions**. This means that oligopolistic firms take into account the likely reactions of their rivals when considering competitive actions such as changing price or implementing new marketing campaigns. It also means that oligopolies are gener-ally large. Oligopolistic markets are common, including industries such as motor vehicle manufacture, television broadcasting and high-street banking. However, a number of high-profile mergers and takeovers in recent years have resulted in these markets containing fewer and larger oligopolies.

Operating in an oligopolistic market has a number of consequences for businesses:
- Such markets are often **highly competitive**.
- Oligopolists **fear price wars** and tend to avoid price competition.
- **Non-price competition** is frequently used (e.g. heavy advertising, loyalty cards such as Tesco's Clubcard and special offers).
- There is a **risk of collusion** whereby producers agree price levels and perhaps output levels. Firms operating together in this way are said to constitute a **cartel**. Such agree-ments are **illegal**.

1.3 Perfect competition

Although near perfectly competitive markets can exist, this is primarily a **theoretical model** of market structure. It is, however, a useful yardstick against which actual markets can be judged. Perfectly competitive markets **have many small firms producing similar products and rely heavily upon price competition**. Firms can enter (and leave) such markets freely. The emphasis on efficient use of resources and price competitiveness allows an interesting comparison with oligopolistic and monopolistic markets.

Categorising markets in this way can help us to predict the likely behaviour of firms in terms of:
- pricing policies
- new product policies
- interdependence or independence
- non-price competition

The ways in which firms compete with one another depend upon the type of market in which they are trading. Thus oligopolies may engage in non-price competition while larger numbers of small businesses are likely to compete in terms of price. When reading the scenario or case study in an examination, make sure you make some assessment of the type of market in which the business is trading.

Markets can be analysed in other ways as well. **One important distinction is the degree of spare capacity existing in the market.** Spare capacity occurs in a market when the firms competing have the ability to produce more than is currently demanded. The existence of spare capacity has a number of implications for firms:

- The excess supply that is available may put downward pressure on prices.
- Firms may find they have surplus labour or other resources.
- The average cost of production may rise and economies of scale may be lost.

Firms can respond in a number of ways to circumstances in which spare or excess capacity exists. These include:

- seeking new markets (possibly overseas) — this is market led
- seeking new uses for existing products — this is product led
- using available capacity to produce different products
- rationalising existing production capacity, perhaps by selling fixed assets and making redundancies
- stockpiling output in the hope of an upturn in sales
- doing nothing, possibly seeing the problem as short term

Questions are frequently set on this area. It is important that you are aware of the implications of spare capacity as well as the responses that firms can make in such a situation. You should consider which of the general responses listed above might be appropriate in the circumstances of any question you are faced with.

2 *Market failure*

Market failure occurs **when the operation of the free market (the interaction of buyers and sellers) results in the inefficient use of resources**. Market failure has a number of characteristics:

- Some important goods, such as education and health, are produced in insufficient quantities.
- There is a growth of monopolies and a reduction in competition.
- There are idle resources, such as unemployed workers and empty factories.
- Large-scale pollution forces those outside the business to bear some of the costs of production.
- Income distribution becomes more uneven.

The government should intervene in cases of market failure to ensure that unemployment is not too high, pollution does not occur, and goods such as health and education are supplied in sufficient quantities.

3 ## Fair and unfair competition

The UK and EU authorities regulate markets with the intention of promoting free and fair competition. They believe this is in the interests of consumers and the inhabitants of the UK and Europe in general. Fair competition exists where firms do not abuse any commercial advantages they may have and do not operate together against the interests of consumers.

Both the UK government and the EU Commission have passed legislation outlawing the following:

- **monopolies that exploit consumers**
- **restrictive practices**, such as firms agreeing to share markets or engaging in full-line forcing (whereby producers 'force' retailers to stock their entire product ranges or refuse to supply and stock them)
- **pricing agreements** among firms (operating a cartel)

For more on legislation designed to promote free and fair competition, see page 157.

B The economy and business

Many students recognise that the economy and the government's economic policies *constrain* business activities, but they fail to appreciate that changes in economic performance and policy often provide *opportunities*. For example, a fall in the exchange value of sterling will make UK exports cheaper overseas. This may offer UK exporters greater opportunities in foreign markets.

All businesses operate within the economy. In fact, the economy comprises tens of thousands of businesses, millions of consumers, local and central governments as well as organisations such as the European Commission. All these individuals and organisations take billions of decisions on, for example, whether to buy, sell, invest, raise prices, lower output and raise interest rates. These interactions comprise the complex entity that is the economy. The behaviour of the economy is a major external influence on businesses.

Examiner's tip
Don't get too bogged down in the detail of economic theory. Of course, it is important to have a broad understanding of issues such as inflation, unemployment, monetary and fiscal policy and the exchange rate. However, it is more important to understand the effects of these factors upon businesses and to be able to analyse a range of possible responses.

1 ## The level of economic activity

The level of economic activity refers to the amount of production, expenditure and employment in the economy. A central measure of the level of economic activity is the level of national income or **gross national product** (GNP).

The level of economic activity is an important factor in assessing the economic environment in which businesses operate (see Table 5.1). The government tries to manipulate the level of economic activity to provide a positive environment for businesses: for example, by attempting to avoid severe booms and slumps in the trade cycle.

Indicators of rising levels of economic activity	Indicators of falling levels of economic activity
Increasing output.	Declining levels of production.
Rising expenditure by consumers and businesses.	Falling expenditure by consumers and businesses.
Tax revenue increases.	Tax revenue declines.
Increased purchases of imports.	Imports may decline.
Greater levels of employment.	Unemployment levels rise.
Build up of inflationary pressure.	Economic growth slows or perhaps becomes negative.
Economic growth sustained and perhaps increasing.	Saving may increase.

Table 5.1 Indicators of rising and falling levels of economic activity

A number of means are available to the government to alter the level of economic activity in the economy, as shown in Table 5.2. (Government policies are considered more fully on pages 168–172.)

Actions to increase the level of economic activity	Actions to reduce the level of economic activity
Reducing direct taxes, such as income tax.	Increasing rates of direct taxes.
Lowering indirect taxes, such as value added tax.	Increasing rates of indirect taxes.
Increasing government expenditure.	Reducing government expenditure.
Implementing policies designed to encourage export sales.	Implementing policies designed to increase savings.
Reducing interest rates.	Increasing interest rates.

Table 5.2 Actions to increase and reduce the level of economic activity

The government manages the economy and alters the level of economic activity in order to achieve a number of objectives. These objectives include:
● steady and sustained economic growth, avoiding the worst booms and slumps associated with the trade cycle
● price stability
● a low rate of unemployment
● a stable exchange rate for the pound sterling

The economic environment for UK businesses is increasingly determined by the actions of the European Union. The creation of the single currency and the introduction of monetary union reflect the growing importance of Europe. This influence will become greater if the UK decides to join the single currency.

2 The trade cycle

The trade cycle, also known as the **business cycle**, describes the regular fluctuations in economic activity occurring over time in all economies. Figure 5.1 illustrates the components of a typical trade cycle.

The trade cycle is a major influence on the performance of businesses for two reasons.
● As the economy moves from one stage of the trade cycle to another, businesses can expect to see substantial changes in their trading conditions.

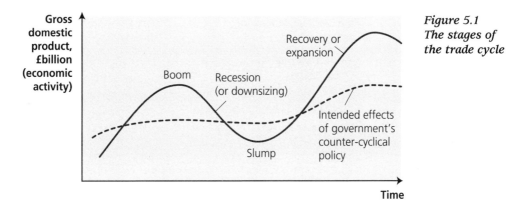

*Figure 5.1
The stages of
the trade cycle*

- The government's economic policies are likely to change along with the stage of the trade cycle to compensate for the alteration of the environment in which businesses are operating.

Figure 5.1 illustrates a smooth and regular trade cycle. In reality, the change in **gross domestic product** (a measure of national income) is likely to be irregular as economic cycles of different duration and intensity operate simultaneously.

Trade cycles generally have four stages (see Table 5.3):

(1) **Upswing or expansion** as the economy recovers from a slump and output and employment rise.
(2) This is followed by **a boom**, with high levels of output and expenditure by firms, consumers and the government.
(3) **A recession** occurs when incomes and output start to fall as demand declines.
(4) **A slump** takes place when output is at its lowest, unemployment is high and increasing numbers of firms go bankrupt.

Stage of the trade cycle	Possible implications for businesses	Possible responses of businesses to changing trading conditions
Upswing or expansion	Rising incomes and expenditures. Labour shortages may occur, pushing up wages. Output may rise, encouraging expansion.	Opportunity to charge higher prices. Adoption of more technology to replace expensive labour. Decide to invest in fixed assets. Operate nearer to full capacity.
Boom	Inflation may rise. Bottlenecks in supply of materials and components. Unable to satisfy levels of demand as consumption rises. Profits are likely to be high.	Face increasing pressure to regularly raise prices. Seek methods to increase output (maybe producing at overseas plants). Wage rises offered to avoid threat of industrial action. Managers plan for falling levels of demand.
Recession	Consumers' disposable incomes start to fall. Demand for many products begins to fall. Some businesses experience financial problems. Excess stocks.	Begin to emphasise price competitiveness in advertising. New markets sought for existing products. Some workers laid off or asked to work short time. Possible reduction in trade credit provided.

Stage of the trade cycle	Possible implications for businesses	Possible responses of businesses to changing trading conditions
Slump	Government may initiate counter-cyclical policies. The number of bankruptcies rises. Increased frequency of bad debts. Government implements counter-cyclical policies: lower interest rates? High levels of unemployment.	Offer basic products at bargain prices. Review credit control policies. Continued targeting of new markets. Seek to diversify product range and sell income inelastic products. Wage levels fall.

Table 5.3 Businesses and the trade cycle

Ideas for application

Not all businesses and products are equally affected by the trade cycle. Firms selling income-elastic products such as antique furniture or foreign holidays are likely to see sales fall as the economy moves into recession. However, retailers of basic foodstuffs or garages selling petrol will remain relatively unaffected.

3 Inflation

Inflation can be defined as a persistent rise in the general level of prices and a corresponding fall in the value of money. The UK government measures the rate of inflation by using the **retail prices index** (RPI). The RPI shows changes in the price of the average person's shopping basket and is calculated through a weighted average of each month's price changes. The greater the proportion of household income spent on an item, the bigger is the effect of any price change on the overall inflation figure. So, for example, if expenditure on food is given a 15% weighting, then rises in food prices will have a substantial impact upon the overall index of inflation.

3.1 The causes of inflation

There are a number of factors that may cause inflation. These causes can be split into two broad groups:

- **Demand-pull inflation.** This occurs when demand for a country's goods and services exceeds its ability to supply these products. Consequently, prices rise as a means of limiting demand to match the available supply. This may be caused by a government allowing firms and individuals to have too much money to spend, perhaps as a result of cutting taxes or lowering interest rates.
- **Cost-push inflation.** This occurs when firms face increasing costs due to factors such as rising wages or higher costs of raw materials and components.

Expectations are an important part of inflation. If businesses anticipate rising inflation, they might take appropriate actions, such as raising their prices in anticipation of higher charges from their suppliers. This will, of course, contribute to inflation.

3.2 The impact of inflation on business

3.2a Adverse effects of inflation

Inflation can have a number of adverse effects on businesses:

- Many businesses may suffer **falling sales** in a period of inflation. Consumers might be expected to spend more during inflationary periods, as they would not wish to hold an asset (money) that is falling in value. However, research shows that people save more (perhaps due to uncertainty) and sales for many businesses fall.
- During periods of high inflation, **governments or central banks tend to raise interest rates** in an attempt to 'cure' the problem. This can lead to a reduction in sales, as consumers are less inclined to borrow money to purchase more expensive items. Sales of new cars might therefore decline.
- It can be **difficult to maintain competitiveness** (especially international competitiveness) during bouts of inflation. Rising wages and raw material costs may force firms to raise prices or accept lower profit margins. Firms operating in countries with lower rates of inflation may gain an edge in terms of price competitiveness under such circumstances.
- Businesses may experience **difficulty in forecasting sales figures and preparing budgets** during periods of high inflation.

3.2b Beneficial effects of inflation

Some analysts suggest that low and stable rates of inflation may be beneficial. A steady rise in profits can create favourable expectations and encourage investment by businesses. Inflation can also encourage long-term borrowing by businesses as the real value of their repayments declines over time.

Some economies, notably Japan, have experienced deflation over recent years. This occurs when prices fall. This can discourage spending and investment in the economy and lead to a reduction in output and prosperity. Firms are discouraged from investing because of the prospect of lower prices for their products, and consumers delay purchases to benefit from lower prices in the future. The Japanese government has experienced great difficulty in stimulating expansion in its economy because of deflation.

The trend in many advanced economies since the mid-1990s has been towards lower levels of inflation and, for some, deflation has become a real possibility.

> **Examiner's tip**
>
> When writing about the impact of inflation and the possible responses of firms, **some consideration of price elasticity** can prove a valuable line of argument. Firms operating in a market where demand is price inelastic are less likely to be affected by rising prices. They can increase prices in order to maintain profit margins.

4 Unemployment

Unemployment exists when those looking for work are unsuccessful in their search. Governments seek to minimise the level of unemployment for a variety of reasons:

- Unemployment is a waste of resources, as people willing to work are kept idle. If 10% of the workforce is unemployed, output is likely to be correspondingly lower.
- Some of the income generated by those in work will need to be diverted to maintain those who are unable to find employment. Those out of work will claim unemployment benefit or may be placed on costly training schemes such as the New Deal.
- Localised unemployment can result in localised poverty as expenditure falls, firms move away or go bankrupt, and the cycle of increased poverty continues.

4.1 Types of unemployment

4.1a Structural unemployment

This is the result of **fundamental changes in the economy**. It may occur because machinery replaces workers, as in the case of bank employees, for whom the use of internet banking has reduced employment. It could also be the result of a decline in the demand for the products of an industry, as in the case of the coal industry.

4.1b Cyclical unemployment

This arises from the operation of the trade cycle. In the boom stage of a trade cycle, this type of unemployment is minimised. At the other extreme, **much of the unemployment experienced during a slump will be cyclical**. This type of unemployment is a major target of the government's counter-cyclical policy.

4.1c Regional unemployment

This reflects **the relative prosperity of the regions of the UK**. Traditionally, Northern Ireland, Scotland, Wales and the north of England have suffered higher rates of regional unemployment than the Midlands and the south of England. The UK government and EU authorities operate regional policies in an attempt to alleviate unemployment black spots, although regional spending by the UK government has declined in recent years.

4.1d Frictional employment

People moving between jobs cause frictional unemployment. Those who leave jobs may not be able to move into new jobs immediately. While they are searching for employment, they are classified as frictionally unemployed.

4.2 Business and changing unemployment levels

Rises in unemployment, actual or forecast, have serious implications for businesses, though the precise impact on firms and their likely responses will depend upon circumstances. For example:

- **Sales might be expected to fall** unless the business is able to add any surplus to stocks or to sell its products in new markets, perhaps overseas.
- If there is a need to reduce output, then **rationalisation and redundancy** might follow. Firms may close subsidiary plants. These actions are unlikely to enhance the corporate image of the business.
- Firms generally **reduce their levels of stock** during a period of high unemployment in an effort to minimise costs. This can add to the need to **reduce current output**.
- **Research and development plans may be abandoned or postponed**, as current levels of demand do not generate enough revenue to finance R&D expenditure.
- The predicted fall in the level of demand may encourage the firm to **diversify**, particularly into goods and services less susceptible to fluctuations in income associated with the trade cycle. **Businesses may consider mergers with other firms** to help reduce costs or to broaden product ranges.

If unemployment falls, the effects are reversed.

The precise policies adopted by a firm when faced with changes in unemployment levels might depend upon factors such as the following:

- **the organisation's size**, financial resources and product range
- **the sensitivity of the business's products** to changes in income levels — that is, its income elasticity
- **the ability of the management team** and its responses to changing circumstances

5   *Interest rates*

5.1   The setting of interest rates

The rate of interest can be described as **the price of borrowed money**. Although we tend to talk of *the* interest rate, there are in fact a range of interest rates operating at any one time. Since May 1997, the Bank of England has had responsibility for setting interest rates. The Bank of England's Monetary Policy Committee (MPC) meets each month and takes decisions on whether to alter interest rates. All other interest rates in the UK economy are based on the rate set by the Bank.

Interest rates in the UK are at a 50-year low of 3.75% at the time of writing (April 2003). Other developed economies have similarly low rates of interest.

5.2   The effects of a rise in interest rates

Changes in interest rates have significant effects on businesses and the environment in which they operate. They are a central part of monetary policy. For more on this, see pages 169–170.

5.2a   Reduced consumer spending

Interest rates affect the level of consumer spending in the economy. A rise in interest rates will normally reduce spending by consumers for a number of reasons:

- Consumers are more likely to take a decision to save during a period in which interest rates are rising. The return on their saving is greater and will persuade some consumers to postpone spending decisions.
- Rising interest rates increase the cost of borrowing. Many goods are purchased on credit, such as electrical goods, cars and caravans, and digital television systems. If rates rise, the cost of purchasing these goods on credit will increase, persuading some people not to buy the product.
- Many UK consumers have mortgages. A rise in interest rates will increase the monthly payments of householders and reduce the income available for other expenditure.

A fall in interest rates will tend to increase demand for many products and expenditure will rise. The reverse of the above will take place.

5.2b   Higher overheads

A rise in interest rates will result in greater overheads for most businesses. For example, a business will encounter greater interest charges on any loans it has taken out. It has been estimated that a 1% rise in interest rates means that small businesses in the UK pay an extra £200 million in interest charges. This could be particularly significant on long-term loans such as mortgages. In times of rising interest rates, firms might limit borrowing (especially short-term borrowing) but may be able to do little about the increased costs of long-term loans.

5.2c   Postponed investment

Firms may postpone investment decisions at a time of rising interest rates. The cost of borrowing money to finance any project is likely to increase when rates rise, and investments may then become unviable. It may become more attractive to place money with a financial institution, since returns may be significantly greater. Postponement of investment decisions reduces the level of economic activity in the economy. The construction and engineering industries are particularly susceptible to declining order books at such a time.

5.2d Higher exchange rate

There is an important link between the domestic rate of interest and the value of a nation's currency. A rise in the UK's rate of interest increases the exchange value of the pound sterling. As interest rates rise in relation to the rates available in other countries, the UK becomes an increasingly attractive target for international investment. Foreigners with money to invest are tempted by the high returns available from UK institutions. However, in order to invest in the UK, foreigners need to purchase pounds. This rise in demand for pounds results in a rise in the exchange rate of the pound. If interest rates fall, the same mechanism operates in reverse (see Table 5.4).

If UK interest rates fall...	If UK interest rates rise...
Foreign investors judge the UK to be a less rewarding place in which to invest their money.	The UK appears a relatively rewarding location for foreign investors to place their funds.
They decide to withdraw existing investments and/or not to make new ones.	Foreign investors decide to invest in UK financial institutions to earn the high rate of interest.
They sell pounds to purchase the currencies of the countries in which they will now invest their funds.	They sell their own currencies to purchase pounds in order to be able to invest in the UK.
The supply of pounds on to the international currency market increases.	The demand for pounds sterling increases on the international currency markets.
The exchange value of the pound falls against other major currencies.	The exchange value of the pound rises against other major currencies.

Table 5.4 The effects of a rise or fall in UK interest rates on the value of the pound

Examiner's tip

Remember that some businesses may benefit during a period of rising interest rates. For example, firms supplying used cars (as opposed to new ones) might experience a rise in sales. Other businesses, such as pawnbrokers, may also benefit.

6 Exchange rates

An exchange rate is **the price of one currency expressed in terms of another**. So, on a given day, one pound may be worth 1.55 US dollars or 1.57 euros.

There is a highly developed foreign exchange market in which currencies are bought and sold. London is one of the premier international centres for exchanging foreign currencies, with transactions totalling billions of pounds each day. Exchange rates between most currencies vary regularly according to the balance of supply and demand for each individual currency.

Currencies are exchanged for a number of reasons:
- **Firms purchasing products from overseas are expected to pay in the producer's domestic currency.** So, a UK firm purchasing Canadian timber will have to change pounds sterling into Canadian dollars to settle its account with the timber exporter, as shown in Figure 5.2.
- Demand for foreign currencies can also arise because **individuals and businesses wish to invest in enterprises overseas**. Thus, a UK citizen wishing to invest in a Japanese business will require yen to complete the transaction.

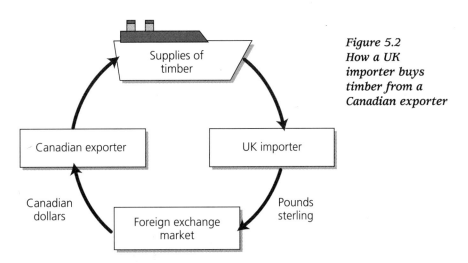

*Figure 5.2
How a UK
importer buys
timber from a
Canadian exporter*

- Sometimes governments buy or sell their own currencies if they wish **to influence the price or exchange rate**. A government decision to use reserves of gold or other foreign currencies to purchase its own currency is likely to increase the exchange rate — provided other people and institutions are not selling huge quantities of the currency. Similarly, selling the currency is likely to depress its exchange value.

6.1 Fixed and floating exchange rates

There are three major ways in which exchange rates can be determined:
- **Freely floating exchange rates.** Most of the world's currencies are allowed to find their values freely on the international foreign exchange markets. Thus, the pound's value is determined by the interaction of supply and demand for the currency. If the UK is judged to be a strong economy and attracts investment from across the globe, then demand for pounds will rise. This is likely to increase the exchange value of the pound.
- **'Dirty' floating.** This occurs when a currency floats but the authorities attempt to influence its value by intervening in the market. Thus, the Japanese government might try to maintain the exchange value of the yen by using its foreign exchange reserves to buy the currency. This can be costly and is usually only a short-term tactic.
- **Fixed exchange rates.** This type of exchange rate system occurs when currencies have a clearly stated and unchanging exchange value. Such a system has allowed the introduction of the EU's single currency, the euro. Eleven EU member countries introduced the euro on 1 January 1999. Prior to this date, the 11 currencies were tied together via a fixed exchange rate system to prepare for the introduction of the euro.

6.2 The effects of exchange rate changes

Changes in exchange rates have a considerable impact upon businesses in the UK. This is true even for those businesses that do not trade overseas. Small changes in the UK's exchange rate occur all the time because it is floating. A series of slight rises and falls over a period of time is not necessarily a major problem for industry. Of more concern is a sustained rise or fall in the exchange rate — or a sudden and substantial change.

Significant changes in the exchange rate can create **a number of difficulties for businesses**:
- Firms experience **difficulty in forecasting earnings from overseas sales** in the event of an exchange rate change taking place in between agreeing the price (in the foreign currency) and receiving payment. If the pound rises in value, then earnings from export sales can decline.

- **Costs of imported raw materials can vary** because of exchange rate fluctuations. A price quoted to customers might suddenly become unprofitable if the price paid for raw materials from overseas rises.
- Significant exchange rate fluctuations can **change the price charged overseas for a product**. A rise in the value of the pound makes it more difficult for exporters, while a fall in the value of the pound can help exporters to be more price competitive.

Example

Norris Engineering exports bicycles to America. Currently they cost £100 to produce and transport to America. With an exchange rate of £1 to $1.50, they can be sold in America for $150 plus the retailer's margin. Following a rise in the value of sterling, the exchange rate is £1 = $1.65. The same bicycle will sell in America for $165 plus the retailer's commission. Sales may fall and Norris Engineering will still receive only £100 for each bicycle sold.

Examiner's tip

When discussing prices (in connection with exchange rates), **do not ignore price elasticity**. If overseas demand for a product is price inelastic, an increase in the exchange rate may not be too harmful. Rolls-Royce's sales might be relatively unaffected in such circumstances. But the same might not be true of a firm selling engineering components in a highly price competitive market.

It is important to be able to analyse the effects of a change in the value of the pound on a business. Table 5.5 summarises these changes.

Exchange value of the pound	Prices of UK exports overseas in local currency	Prices of products imported into the UK in pounds sterling
Increases (appreciates)	Rise	Fall
Decreases (depreciates)	Fall	Rise

Table 5.5 The effects on a business of a change in the value of the pound

Changes in exchange rates only affect the price at which imports and exports are sold. A number of other factors influence purchasing decisions in international markets:
- the reputation and quality of the product in question
- the design and functions of the product
- the after-sales service provided
- delivery dates and the business's record in meeting them

Ideas for application

Exchange rates are an important issue for businesses selling in price competitive international markets. In these circumstances, a small change in the exchange rate can eliminate a firm's profit margin or make the firm uncompetitive.

C Business and law

The European Union and the UK government play a major role in determining the environment in which firms operate, by implementing a range of legislation that affects businesses. The EU has an increasing role in passing laws (known as **directives**) that influence the activities of UK businesses. In the case of any conflict between EU and UK law, the legislation of the European Union takes precedence.

The key areas of legislation that affect business are:
- competition policy
- health and safety
- employment protection
- consumer protection

Examiner's tip

It is important in this area of the specification to concentrate on the impact of legislation on businesses and their possible responses to changes in the legal environment. Do not spend long periods learning the content of the various laws. A broad appreciation of the nature and scope of the relevant legislation is all that is required.

1 Competition policy

Competition policy deals with monopolies, mergers and restrictive practices. A monopoly can be defined as 'a situation where there are no close substitutes for the goods that a firm produces'. The result of monopolies could be that:
- consumers are exploited through excessive prices
- consumers are offered a poor service
- some firms face unfair competition

A number of safeguards against such exploitation exist. These include:
- **Greater competition.** For example, since privatisation British Telecom (BT) has not had a monopoly in supplying telephone equipment.
- **The formation of 'watchdog' organisations**, such as OFTEL, which monitors complaints from BT customers.
- **The Office of Fair Trading and the Competition Commission.** These bodies ensure that firms with a large share of the market do not act against the public interest; proposed mergers are investigated, competition is encouraged and restrictive practices are discouraged. The Competition Commission was previously called the Monopolies and Mergers Commission.
- **The Restrictive Practices Court.** This considers cases involving restrictive practices (i.e. business practices that reduce the degree of competition): for example, creating cartels that set high prices or other adverse conditions of sale.
- **The Data Protection Act (1984).** This is designed to prevent businesses abusing the power and access to information which computers and databases give them. It is most applicable to information processed by computer. Such data cannot be used or disclosed in any manner incompatible with the purpose for which the information is held.

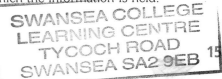

2 Health and safety legislation

Health and safety legislation has been enacted **to discourage dangerous practices by businesses and to protect the workforce**. The legislation focuses on the prevention of accidents. The main act in the UK is the **Health and Safety at Work Act (1974)**. This is an example of delegated legislation, whereby Parliament delegates responsibility to government departments to produce 'statutory instruments' to update the scope of the legislation as necessary. This ensures that legislation is relevant while not taking up too much of Parliament's time.

Examiner's tip

You should be aware of the key terms in this area of the specification. Terms worthy of research include: **cartels**, **restrictive practices**, **voluntary codes of practice** and **oligopolies**. Understanding important terms allows you to answer definition questions with confidence, but also to use these words as a form of shorthand when developing analytical and evaluative answers.

The main provisions of the Health and Safety at Work Act are designed to 'ensure as far as is reasonably practical' the health and safety of all staff at work. The provisions of the act include the following:
- All employees are obliged to follow safety rules and regulations.
- Firms must display a written safety policy.
- Businesses should provide necessary safety equipment free of charge.
- Safety representatives have the right to investigate workplace accidents and conduct the inspections necessary to ensure a safe workplace.

The UK's health and safety legislation is continuously updated under the provisions of the Health and Safety at Work Act to take account of changes in working practices. For example, in December 2002 health and safety legislation relating to explosive substances in the workplace was strengthened following a number of accidents.

In addition, the European Union has enacted health and safety legislation relating to pregnant workers, the length of the working week and the use of computers in the workplace.

Ideas for application

Health and safety legislation is an important issue for firms operating in the primary and secondary sectors of the economy. For example, construction companies impose rigorous health and safety policies and monitor incidents very closely to avoid their repetition.

3 Employment protection

Employment protection falls into two categories:
- individual labour law
- collective labour law

3.1 Individual labour law

This category of legislation **grants protection to, and places obligations on, individuals**.

Some key pieces of legislation are as follows:

- Discrimination on grounds of sex in employment and education is unlawful under the **Sex Discrimination Acts (1975, 1986)** as reinforced by the **Employment Act (1989)**.
- The **Equal Pay Act (1970)** states that sexes should be treated equally. A woman employed in the same job as a man must have the same pay and conditions of employment.
- The **Race Relations Act (1976)** makes it unlawful to discriminate in relation to employment on the grounds of sex, marital status, colour or race.
- The **Disability Discrimination Act (1995)** makes it illegal for an employer to treat a disabled person less favourably than others.
- The **National Minimum Wage Act (1998)** is a highly publicised act that came into force on 1 April 1999. The key features of the new legislation are a general minimum wage of £4.20 per hour and a minimum level of £3.60 an hour for 18–21-year-olds (2002 rates). All part-time and temporary workers must be paid the minimum wage.
- The **Working Time Regulations (1998)** are European Union legislation, limiting the hours that employees can be required to work each week to 48 hours. Employees can choose to work longer hours, but employers cannot insist that they do so without inserting an appropriate clause in their contract of employment.

3.2 Collective labour law

This legislation relates to **industrial relations and trade union activities**. The relevant pieces of recent legislation are outlined below.

3.2a The Employment Protection (Consolidation) Act (1978)

This covers a number of aspects:

- **Contracts of employment.** All employees working more than 16 hours per week must be given a contract of employment by their employer within 13 weeks of starting work.
- **Dismissal of employees.** Once employed for 4 weeks, employees are entitled to a minimum of 1 week's notice. After 2 years, this increases to a period of 1 week for each year's service up to a maximum of 12 weeks.
- **Dismissal procedures.** Normally an employee is given a verbal warning of unsatisfactory conduct or performance followed by a written warning if appropriate. If the problem remains, there may be a formal hearing at which the employee may be represented by his or her trade union.

3.2b Industrial relations legislation

A whole series of legislation has been passed, starting with the **Industrial Relations Act (1971)**, to influence negotiations between employers and employees. These have included the following acts:

- **Employment Act (1980).** This enabled firms to derecognise unions. It also restricted picketing to employees' 'own place of work'.
- **Employment Act (1982).** This placed further restrictions on lawful industrial action and meant that trade unions could be sued for implementing unlawful industrial action.
- **Trade Union Act (1984).** This made a secret ballot of employees mandatory before industrial action was lawful.
- **Employment Act (1988).** This protected union members from being disciplined by unions for ignoring strike calls.
- **Employment Act (1990).** This reduced the likelihood of unofficial strikes by permitting employers to dismiss workers taking this form of action. The act effectively ended

closed-shop agreements. It made it illegal to refuse to employ an individual because he or she is not a member of a union.

- **Trade Union Reform and Employment Rights Act (1993).** This required unions to provide employers with at least 7 days' notice of official industrial action. It also abolished wages councils and their imposition of minimum pay rates.
- **Employment Relations Act (1999).** This established legal guidelines for union recognition by employers in businesses with over 21 employees as well as granting up to 3 months' parental leave to mothers and fathers. Finally, in a minor reversal of some earlier legislation, it extended the legal protection given to workers taking industrial action.

3.3 Industrial tribunals

These were established in 1964 and face a constantly heavy workload. They sit locally to hear complaints by employees about:
- contracts of employment
- unfair dismissal
- redundancy
- sex and race discrimination
- equal pay

4   Consumer protection

Consumer protection encompasses a series of acts designed to safeguard consumers against unfair trading practices and dangerous products. This is managed by the **Office of Fair Trading**, which also looks after competition policy. The legislation already in place is outlined below.

4.1 Sale of Goods Act (1979)

The basic requirement is that the seller must ensure that the goods sold are satisfactory. They must be:
- of merchantable quality — that is, they must be undamaged and unbroken, and must work properly
- fit for the particular purpose
- as described by the manufacturer

4.2 Consumer Protection Act (1987)

This act means that producers can be held liable for harm caused by their products.

4.3 Other acts

- **Food Safety Act (1990)** — to ensure the safety of food.
- **Trade Descriptions Act (1968)** — misleading descriptions of goods/services are an offence.
- **Weights and Measures (1963) and (1985)** — weights and measures given must be accurate.
- **Consumer Credit Act (1974)** — credit can be given only by licensed organisations.

4.4 Control of advertising

This is necessary to protect the public from improper use of the power of advertising. Protection takes the form of a combination of legal controls and self-regulation.

- **The Code of Advertising Practice Committee.** Made up of representatives of the trade associations involved in advertising, this committee is responsible for preparing, amending and enforcing a code of practice for advertisers.
- **The Advertising Standards Authority (ASA).** This body supervises the operation of the Code of Advertising Practice. It is an independent body; its members are not in the advertising industry. The ASA protects the public interest and deals with complaints from the public.

Increases in the scope of consumer protection have had a number of **implications for businesses**:
- **The costs of production have risen.** Meeting the requirements of, for example, weights and measures and consumer credit entails additional processes and personnel, thereby increasing costs.
- **There is greater emphasis on supplying products of consistently high quality.** Firms are vulnerable to prosecution for supplying substandard items and wish to avoid any adverse publicity in this respect.
- **Consumerism is now a force to be reckoned with.** Consumers have become more knowledgeable and discerning in their purchases. They often conduct research (aided by publications such as *Which?*) before making major purchases.

D Social opportunities and constraints

Social factors have a considerable impact on the behaviour of businesses. Over recent years, many changes in social attitudes have been highlighted by the activities of pressure groups. Important issues have included:
- the desire among consumers to purchase environmentally friendly products
- increasing concern expressed about the treatment of farm animals and a greater number of consumers opting to become vegetarians
- a demand for firms to meet the needs of other groups apart from shareholders
- the increasing number of single-person households and their different patterns of demand

A business's social responsibilities are the duties it has towards its stakeholders — employees, customers and society at large — as well as towards its shareholders (see Figure 5.3). Some firms willingly embrace these responsibilities, while others reject them.

Those who support the **stakeholder concept** recognise that a business has to aim to satisfy the needs of all groups that have an interest in the organisation. The **shareholder concept** argues that businesses exist to meet the needs of shareholders for profits and that decisions should reflect this objective.

A business may accept its social responsibilities for two reasons:
- It has a genuine belief in the stakeholder concept, which recognises the needs of all parties with an interest in the organisation.
- It believes that it can derive some positive publicity from being seen to be socially responsible.

Figure 5.3
The stakeholders of a business

Increasingly, firms are being asked to consider and justify their actions towards a wide range of groups rather than just their shareholders. A number of issues arise as a result of these pressures:

- Even firms that have a genuine desire to change may experience difficulties in altering the existing culture. It may take years to establish a genuine stakeholder culture.
- The stakeholder approach can lead to many benefits for organisations. These include: keeping existing customers and winning new ones; recruiting and keeping high-quality employees; and developing a positive long-term corporate image.
- The precise social responsibilities that a firm should meet vary from business to business and change over time. However, consumers increasingly expect businesses to meet their social responsibilities.

It is unlikely that a business will be able to meet the needs of all interest groups. It is normal for some sort of trade-off to take place. By fulfilling the needs of one stakeholder group, the demands of others may be ignored. In a time of slump, when profits are reduced, businesses may be more likely to focus on meeting the needs of shareholders. In more prosperous periods, a broader range of stakeholders may be satisfied.

Ideas for application

Social responsibilities are particularly important for some types of business. For example, firms producing relatively undifferentiated products may opt to meet social responsibilities as fully as possible in order to provide a unique selling proposition.

E Business ethics

1 Definition

Ethics can be defined as a code of behaviour considered morally correct. Business ethics can provide moral guidelines for decision making by organisations. Taking an ethical decision means doing what is morally right. It is not simply taking the decision that leads to the highest profits. Many activities in the business world have an ethical dimension. Here are some examples:

- Should a manufacturing business use a cheap, non-sustainable source of timber or a more expensive, sustainable supply that would mean lower profits for shareholders?
- Should a retail chain recruit and train employees or simply poach them from a rival business by offering slightly higher wages?
- If a business is faced by declining demand, should it make its workers redundant immediately or consider retraining them or seeing whether demand picks up in the near future?
- Should a distributor accept a profitable contract to transport tobacco products in the knowledge that they are damaging to the health of the public?

The actions underpinning these questions are not illegal, but many people would regard them as morally wrong (see Figure 5.4). Whether a business would turn down profitable (or cost-saving) opportunities such as these is debatable.

Figure 5.4
The law and ethical behaviour by businesses

2 Business ethics versus the law

The law protects society from the worst excesses of business behaviour. Thus, competition legislation prevents monopolies abusing their power and employment protection legislation looks after the welfare of workers. Ethical behaviour requires businesses to take this process a step further.

Ethical or morally acceptable behaviour requires businesses to reject potentially profitable activities because they have an unacceptable dimension. A food manufacturer, for example, might decide not to use supplies of genetically modified flour in bread, even though traditional sources are significantly more expensive. It would not be illegal to use the genetically modified materials, but the directors of the business may not consider this a morally correct course of action. Ethical behaviour offers benefits to business as well as imposing additional costs, as shown in Table 5.6.

Advantages	Disadvantages
There are obvious benefits to a business that is perceived by the public as ethically correct. This may result in increased sales.	Taking ethical decisions can be expensive. It may involve turning down highly profitable trading opportunities in favour of taking moral decisions.
Having a positive ethical stance may assist a business in recruiting high-quality employees. It may also result in a lower turnover of staff.	There may be conflict with existing staff or existing policies. For example, a policy of delegation may pose problems when attempting to promote a more ethical culture.

Table 5.6 Advantages and disadvantages of ethical behaviour

F Technological change

Technology is advancing at an ever-increasing rate and affects both processes and products. Technological developments include:

- more advanced and sophisticated computers
- the internet
- third-generation (3G) mobile telephones
- computer-aided design (CAD) and computer-aided manufacture (CAM)

As the list above shows, technological advances have created new products, new ways of producing products and new ways of selling products. For example, changes in technology mean that more powerful and technologically sophisticated computers are manufactured regularly. But advances in technology mean that computers can be sold in different ways. One of the world's leading manufacturers, Dell, sells its products via the internet rather than through high street retailers. This keeps costs to a minimum, boosting profitability.

Developments in technology have dramatically improved the process of production for many firms — services as well as manufacturing. The development of computer-aided design (CAD) has made the design of new products easier to carry out, store and to alter. Modern software can also be used to estimate the cost of newly designed products. Technology has revolutionised manufacturing too. Computer-aided manufacturing is used by manufacturing firms of all sizes. Computers control the machines on the production line, saving labour and costs, and CAM systems can be linked to CAD technology to transform the entire process.

1 Benefits of new technology

New technology offers businesses and consumers a range of benefits:

- **Reduced unit costs of production**, enhancing the competitiveness of the business concerned. For example, Boeing, the American aircraft manufacturer, designs much of its new aircraft on computers and can assemble 'virtual aircraft'. This reduces the company's use of expensive prototypes.
- In the case of high-technology products, such as new games consoles, the **opportunity to charge a premium price** until the competition catches up. Such price skimming is likely to boost profits.
- **New markets**: for example, the internet allows online bookshops to sell worldwide.

2 Costs of new technology

New technology also poses difficulties for many businesses. For example:

- It is likely to be a **drain on an organisation's capital**. In some circumstances (for example, when experiencing high gearing), firms may experience difficulty in raising the funds necessary to install high-technology equipment or to research a new product.
- It inevitably **requires training** of the existing workforce and perhaps **recruitment** of new employees. Both actions can create considerable costs for businesses.
- Its introduction may be met with **opposition** from existing employees, especially if job security is threatened. This may lead to industrialisation.

A2 External influences

This section builds upon the material covered at AS. It is recommended that you re-read the AS materials alongside those that follow. Although A2 questions will focus on the following topics, it is likely that some of the principles covered at AS will be needed to support your answers.

A Economic influences on business strategy

A business's strategy is the medium- to long-term plan that it uses to achieve its overall (or corporate) objectives. Corporate objectives might include goals such as increasing market share or diversification. A business's ability to achieve its corporate objectives is likely to be influenced by the economic environment in which it trades. Thus, changes in interest rates, exchange rates, inflation, unemployment and the trade cycle may all have an impact on a firm's strategy.

1 Interest rates and exchange rates

1.1 Interest rates

The Labour government that has been in power since May 1997 has used interest rates as a central part of its economic policy. There have been many changes in rates over the years with the general trend being for interest rates to decline.

Changes in interest rates have substantial implications for businesses. A fall in rates will make businesses more likely to invest in new productive capacity. Lower rates make borrowing for expansion cheaper and increase the probability of any project returning a profit. At the same time, consumer spending is likely to increase in these circumstances as the cost of credit declines. Finally, a fall in interest rates is likely to depress the value of the pound, reducing the price of exports and providing a boost for UK firms selling overseas.

Declining rates of interest are likely to encourage firms to implement expansionary strategies, such as takeovers and entering new markets. However, businesses take a long-term view when deciding upon strategy and interest rates can change quickly. If managers believe that interest rates are volatile, they may not base their strategy upon such a changeable variable.

1.2 Exchange rates

Exchange rates can create uncertainty among businesses for a number of reasons:
- Firms may receive different revenues from those expected from international transactions because of changes in exchange rates. This may reduce (or even eliminate) profits from a deal.
- Costs of raw materials and components may change because of movements in exchange rates. This can make the process of budgeting more difficult.

A number of groups have criticised the desire for continual economic growth. At the centre of their arguments is the damage that economic growth inflicts on the environment. Individuals and pressure groups, such as Greenpeace and Friends of the Earth, argue that continual economic growth causes environmental problems including:

- global warming
- acid rain
- depletion of the ozone layer
- disposing of vast amounts of waste

Governments throughout the world are implementing policies designed to balance the needs of the environment against the desire of their citizens to enjoy higher standards of living. Some governments come under more pressure from environmental activists than others, but the international nature of some environmental pressure groups means that few governments can afford to be seen allowing businesses to damage the environment with impunity.

B Government policies to control the economy

The government implements a series of policies designed to provide a **stable and prosperous economic environment for businesses**. Successive governments have argued that an appropriate economic environment would show the following characteristics:

- steady and sustained economic growth, avoiding the worst booms and slumps associated with the trade cycle
- price stability
- low rates of unemployment
- a stable exchange rate for the pound

1 Fiscal policy

Fiscal policy refers to government policies based on taxation and its own expenditure.

1.1 Taxation

The UK has two broad categories of taxes:

- **direct taxes**, levied on income and capital (e.g. income tax)
- **indirect taxes**, levied on expenditure (e.g. value added tax)

The government can raise the level of economic activity in the UK by lowering the rates of taxation. The Chancellor of the Exchequer usually announces changes in the rates of taxation during the Budget speech. The effects of such changes are outlined in Table 5.8.

It is relatively easy to forecast the impact of changes in taxation rates on the overall level of economic activity. The effects of these changes vary between individual firms. **Businesses producing price-elastic goods will be affected by changes in indirect taxes, as demand is sensitive to price. Those firms producing income-elastic products may find their sales more affected by alterations in the rates of direct taxation.** Firms supplying products such as foreign holidays or jewellery will be sensitive to changes in consumers' incomes; those selling basic foodstuffs are less likely to be affected.

The effects of increases in taxation	The effects of reductions in taxation
Increases in indirect taxes such as VAT result in higher prices, cutting consumer demand.	Cutting indirect taxes reduces prices, which may boost spending — especially for price-elastic products.
Producers may pay the increase in indirect taxes to avoid raising prices; this will cut profits and may reduce investment levels by businesses.	Reductions in income tax result in consumers having higher levels of disposable income. This increases demand, particularly for income-elastic products.
Increases in income tax leave consumers with less disposable income, again reducing demand.	Falling corporate taxation promotes investment and output by businesses, increasing economic activity.
A rise in corporate taxation reduces business profits, contributing to a fall in investment and output.	Reductions in corporate taxation may attract inward investment by foreign individuals and businesses, promoting prosperity.

Table 5.8 The effects of increases and reductions in taxation

1.2 Government expenditure

Government expenditure is the other part of fiscal policy. It can be placed in two categories:

- **Transfer payments.** This is government spending on pensions, unemployment benefit and similar social security payments. Alterations in this category of government expenditure have a rapid and significant impact on consumers' spending and the level of economic activity. Recipients are generally not well off and need to spend the money to maintain their standard of living.
- **Spending on the nation's infrastructure.** This is spending on such things as roads, schools, bridges and harbours. This type of expenditure can have a double impact upon businesses. First, the results of the expenditure can enhance the environment for firms by improving communications and cutting the costs of transportation. Second, the construction can provide work and income for firms, so boosting their profitability. The government can also encourage investment by companies through offering investment grants and tax relief (see Table 5.9).

	Falling level of economic activity	Rising level of economic activity
Caused by	Reduced government spending or increased taxation.	Increased government expenditure or lower rates of taxation.
Likely effects	Increased unemployment, declining spending and production.	Inflation may appear whilst unemployment falls as imports increase.
Impact on business	Falling sales and downward pressure on prices. Rising numbers of bankruptcies, especially amongst small firms. Increased stock levels.	Rising wages and possible skill shortages. Sales rise and possibility of increasing prices. Increasing costs of raw materials and components.

Table 5.9 Fiscal policy and levels of economic activity

2 *Monetary policy*

This method of controlling the economy centres on adjusting the amount of money in circulation and hence the level of spending and economic activity. Monetary policy can make use of one or more of the following:

- altering interest rates

- controlling the money supply
- manipulating the exchange rate

Although at times all three techniques have been used, recent governments have tended to adopt neutral fiscal policies and to rely on adjusting interest rates to manage the economy. We saw under the heading 'Interest rates' (page 153) that interest rate policy has been controlled by the Monetary Policy Committee of the Bank of England since 1997.

Broadly speaking, rises in interest rates depress the level of economic activity and reductions promote an expansion of economic activity.

A rise in the level of interest rates in the UK will reduce the level of economic activity for a number of reasons:

- Individuals and businesses will tend to save more, so reducing the level of expenditure and production.
- Consumers will postpone or abandon plans to purchase goods on credit, as interest charges have risen.
- Businesses will take decisions to reduce investment plans, as the cost of borrowing has risen and fewer projects will be viable.
- Firms may reduce stock levels in an attempt to reduce their need to borrow to obtain working capital.
- Trade credit will become more expensive and firms will seek to offer less credit (at the same time as they attempt to gain more).
- There may be upward pressure on costs, as firms face higher charges to service their long-term debt. This may result in increases in retail prices.
- Firms may encounter (and have to make provision for) higher levels of bad debts.
- There will be an increase in the exchange value of the pound through the mechanism outlined earlier. This will increase the price of UK exports while reducing the price of imports.

The impact of rising interest rates will depend upon the size of the change as well as the initial rate. A small increase at a relatively high level of rates will have little impact, while a larger increase from a low base rate will have a significant impact. As the economies of the European Union become more integrated, EU interest rates will become more influential on the behaviour of businesses.

Ideas for application

Demand for some products is sensitive to changes in interest rates. They could be said to be interest elastic. For example, houses, furniture and cars fall into this category, as they are frequently purchased on credit.

3 Supply-side policies

Policies designed to promote greater and more efficient production have gained credence over recent years. **They attempt to improve the working of the economy by improving the operation of free markets.**

The main elements of supply-side policies are:

- **Improving the quality of the labour force.** This can be done through increasing training to provide a more committed and skilled labour force. The Investors in People (IIP) scheme is an integral part of this approach.
- **Limiting the power of trade unions.** One reason for restricting the power of trade unions has been to make the labour market work more effectively and to avoid the excessive wage increases and limited increases in productivity that some people associate with the exercise of trade union power.
- **Reducing labour costs.** By making the labour market work effectively, the government hopes to allow wages to reflect local conditions. However, the introduction of the minimum wage in 1999 has imposed an artificial constraint on the operation of labour markets.

4 Intervention versus laissez-faire approaches to economic management

4.1 The move to laissez faire

We noted above that governments have recently begun to rely more heavily upon the free operation of markets. This move reflects **a change in the economic philosophy of successive governments**, as they have taken the view that limited intervention in the economy is the most effective means of promoting prosperity. The increasing reliance on the free operation of markets reflects a more laissez-faire (literally 'leave alone') attitude on the part of the authorities.

A laissez-faire policy means that governments tax less and spend less on supporting businesses and providing state services to businesses. This approach places faith in businesses operating a degree of self-regulation. The respective benefits of this approach and the interventionist approach are shown in Table 5.10.

Benefits of a laissez-faire approach to economic management	Benefits of intervention as a central part of economic management
Reduced levels of direct taxation.	Governments protect and support 'lame ducks', maintaining employment, especially in depressed regions.
Less bureaucracy interfering with and imposing extra costs on businesses.	Employees are less vulnerable to the actions of unscrupulous employers.
Wages and other costs may fall in poorer regions, making them more attractive to businesses.	
Foreign businesses may invest in the UK economy because of its limited regulations and low rates of tax.	Consumers gain the full protection of the law and do not suffer from high prices or substandard products.
Government funds can be switched to other targets, such as improving the mobility and skills of the labour force.	The government ensures that businesses do not abuse their monopoly power.

Table 5.10 Laissez-faire versus interventionist approaches to economic management

4.2 Privatisation

One aspect of recent economic management that reflects the move towards a more laissez-faire stance is the policy of privatisation. Throughout the world, governments have sold industries previously run by the state to private individuals and businesses. This has given businesses the opportunity to compete in areas of the economy that were previously dominated by a public monopoly.

However, since the late 1990s the criticisms of the policy of privatisation have become louder. The improved quality of services promised from privatisation of industries such as the railways has not been realised. Government plans to privatise the London Underground and air traffic control have encountered vociferous opposition.

C The European Union

1 Origins

The origins of the European Union (EU) lie in the creation of the European Coal and Steel Community (ECSC) in 1952. This was the first of a number of stages along the road towards the establishment of the EU and the single currency:

1952 The Treaty of Paris is signed by Belgium, the Netherlands, Luxembourg, Italy, France and (later) West Germany to establish the European Coal and Steel Community (ECSC).

1957 The same six countries sign the Treaty of Rome and create the European Economic Community (EEC).

1967 The EEC amalgamates with the ECSC and the resulting body is called the European Community (EC). This amalgamation confirms the original objective of the Treaty of Rome — to remove all trade barriers between the member states.

1973 Britain, Ireland and Denmark join the EC.

1986 Greece becomes a member of the EC.

1990 Spain and Portugal take the EC's membership to 12.

1991 In the small Dutch town of Maastricht, the Treaty of European Union is signed by all the member states to take effect on 1 November 1993. This treaty creates the European Union with the aim of even greater unity between member states, including monetary union.

1996 Sweden, Finland and Austria become members.

1999 On 1 January, a single European currency, the euro, is adopted by 11 member states.

2002 The EU agrees to admit ten new member states by 2004.

In 2003 member states of the European Union were: Austria, Belgium, Denmark, Finland, France, Germany, Greece, Ireland, Italy, Luxembourg, the Netherlands, Portugal, Spain, Sweden and the United Kingdom. In 2004 they will be joined by Cyprus, the Czech Republic, Estonia, Hungary, Latvia, Lithuania, Malta, Poland, Slovakia and Slovenia.

2 The institutions of the European Union

2.1 The European Commission

The commission proposes EU policy and legislation, which is then considered by the Council of Ministers. It also carries out the decisions taken by the Council of Ministers. Each EU member state provides commissioners — two each from France, Germany, Italy, Spain and the UK, and one from each of the remaining member states. However, it is probable that each country will provide a single commissioner after May 2004.

2.2 The Council of the European Union

The council agrees or adopts legislation on the basis of proposals from the European Commission. Each member state acts as President of the Council for 6 months. Meetings are held four times a year and one minister from each state attends. Heads of government meet twice yearly in the European Council and establish guidelines for future EU policies.

2.3 The European Parliament

The European Parliament has 626 members (Members of the European Parliament or MEPs); 87 from the UK. However, this pattern will change following enlargement in May 2004. The parliament's opinion is needed on proposals before the European Commission can implement them. The European Parliament has relatively little power.

2.4 The European Court of Justice

The Court of Justice is staffed with one judge from each member state. The court rules on interpretation and application of EU legislation. It ensures that the law established by the Treaty of Rome is observed and deals with disputes between member states.

3 Opportunities and threats for UK business

The establishment and enlargement of the European Union has created opportunities for UK businesses at the same time as it has posed threats to the same firms. It has required considerable changes in strategy by those firms that trade across the European continent as well as by those merely subject to new and fiercer competition.

3.1 Opportunities

The opportunities offered by the European Union include the following:

- UK businesses operate in **a home market with over 450 million consumers** (larger than the USA and Japan combined), offering scope for considerable economies of scale and increased profits.
- The scale of the European market means that firms can specialise in particular **niche markets** and earn sufficient profits.
- Firms trading throughout the EU can seek **mergers and commercial agreements** with other European businesses. Organisations can derive benefits by cooperating with businesses whose strengths are complementary. Alternatively, **takeovers** might be the means by which businesses increase their scale to cope with the European market.
- The opening up of the European market offers UK businesses **new, and possibly cheaper, sources of supply**. Operating in a larger, more competitive European market will drive down the costs of raw materials and components. The **free movement of workers** also makes potentially cheaper sources of labour available, especially from eastern Europe.

3.2 Threats

- UK businesses face **much more competition** from European businesses, even in the United Kingdom. This can result in prices being forced down, giving lower profit margins or even resulting in bankruptcy.
- Some UK businesses may be liable to **hostile takeovers** by larger European businesses intent on dominating the new European market.

In response to questions on objectives and strategy you should be prepared to draw on subject knowledge from across the specification. This chapter covers a number of important aspects of business activity. It considers the nature and importance of business objectives and the potential for conflict among those who have an interest in a business. It then goes on to look at how small businesses are established and developed. Finally, it considers business strategy. Strategy is the medium- to long-term plan necessary to achieve a corporate objective. Such plans are developed at a senior level in an organisation. This chapter also looks at decision-making techniques designed to help managers and directors develop their strategies.

AS Objectives and strategy

The three specifications cover similar topics, such as aims and objectives, the legal structure of businesses and stakeholder analysis. However, there are some differences between the AS specifications for AQA, Edexcel and OCR. The AQA and Edexcel specifications emphasise small businesses and include sections on identifying business opportunities and starting a business. The OCR specification does not include this. AQA has mission statements as part of its A2 specification, but it is included here in the AS specification, as it fits naturally alongside aims and objectives.

A Introduction

Businesses in the UK — or any other economy — can be divided into three sectors.
- The **primary sector** comprises those industries concerned with growing natural products and extracting mineral resources.
- The **secondary sector** includes business involved in manufacturing and construction, often using products from the primary sector.
- The **tertiary sector** is made up of businesses providing services.

1 The primary sector

Businesses in the primary sector grow crops or extract raw materials. This sector includes agriculture, fishing, forestry, mining and quarrying. Many firms in the primary sector are relatively small, particularly in agriculture and fishing. However, it is more common for firms in fuel extraction, mining and quarrying to be large. For example, British Coal employs over 8,000 people and produces over 21 million tonnes of coal each year.

2 The secondary sector

Secondary production covers manufacturing and construction. This includes a wide range of industries, such as house building, food processing and car manufacture. The secondary sector has changed dramatically as foreign manufacturing firms like Sony and Nissan have moved to the UK. Furthermore, new technology has transformed the activities of

many businesses in the secondary sector. Developments in technology have caused the decline of some traditional industries while creating new ones, such as computer manufacturing.

3 The tertiary sector

Tertiary production is concerned with service industries. This is the largest sector of the economy, including retailing, financial services, education, health care, leisure, transport and communications. The UK has a worldwide reputation for providing certain services, notably banking and insurance.

4 The move towards tertiary production

Table 6.1 shows that the UK has moved away from primary and secondary production, while the tertiary sector has become hugely important. The use of technology in the primary and secondary sectors means that output has not fallen in line with employment, but the tertiary sector accounted for over 60% of output in 2001.

Industrial sector	1901	1951	1971	1981	1998
Primary sector (e.g. mining)	14.0	9.0	4.5	3.3	1.4
Secondary sector (e.g. manufacturing)	39.5	44.1	42.7	34.9	22.6
Tertiary sector (services)	40.0	47.0	52.8	61.8	76.1

Source: Adapted from www.statistics.gov.uk.

Table 6.1 Percentage employment in primary, secondary and tertiary sectors, 1901–98

B Business objectives

1 Mission statements

Mission statements summarise a business's long-term aims and are intended to provide the organisation with a sense of common purpose. Organisations attempt to encapsulate the purpose of their existence in a single sentence, which represents its vision or mission. Coca-Cola says that its mission is to 'get more people to drink Coke than water'. This reflects its mission to dominate the market.

Mission statements focus on:
- corporate values
- non-financial objectives
- benefits of the business to the community
- how consumers are to be satisfied

Figure 6.1 shows the hierarchy of objectives stemming from a mission statement.

2 Corporate aims

Aims are long-term plans from which company objectives are derived. They do not normally state targets in numerical terms. From these aims or mission statements, a

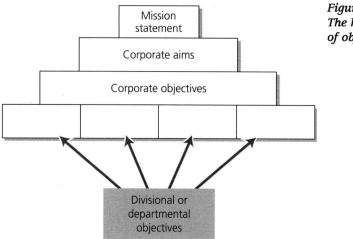

Figure 6.1
The hierarchy
of objectives

company can set quantifiable objectives, such as gaining market leadership in Europe within 3 years.

3   Company objectives

Business objectives are medium- to long-term goals established to coordinate the business. Objectives should be quantified and have a stated timescale, such as to earn a 20% return on capital next year.

Companies may have a number of objectives and these are considered below.

3.1 Survival

This is an important objective:

- for small businesses, particularly in their first few years
- during periods of recession or intense competition
- at a time of crisis, such as during a hostile takeover bid

3.2 Profit maximisation

Profits are maximised when **the difference between sales revenue and total costs is at its greatest**. Some firms seek to earn the greatest possible profits to satisfy their shareholders' desire for high dividends. Others are content to pursue a satisfactory level of profit. Known as **satisficing**, this is common among small firms where higher profits may require the entrepreneur to work excessive hours.

3.3 Growth

Many businesses pursue growth because their managers believe that the organisation will not survive otherwise. If a firm grows, it should be able to exploit its market position and earn higher profits. This benefits shareholders (in the long term) by providing greater dividends as well as offering better salaries and more job security to the employees and managers of the business.

3.4 Managerial objectives

Managers can pursue their own objectives rather than those set by the owners (shareholders). Managerial objectives might include the following:

- maximising leisure time

- maximising financial rewards — pension, bonuses and salary
- seeking to take over rival companies
- establishing modern working practices
- improving professional status

3.5 Corporate image

This has become a more important objective for many companies recently. Companies fear that consumers who have a negative view of them will not purchase their products. This applies to any action that damages the company image.

The objectives pursued by a business vary according to its size, ownership and legal structure. This is illustrated in Table 6.2.

Objective	Corner shop	Partnership	Small local company	Bernard Matthews	Eastern Electricity	Shell
Survival	✔	✔	✔			
Profit maximisation			✔	✔		✔
Growth		✔	✔	✔	✔	✔
Diversification					✔	✔
Corporate image				✔	✔	✔

Table 6.2 Businesses and objectives

Ideas for application

Think how a business's objectives might alter as its circumstances change. Thus, for example, survival might be important to a newly established firm, profits to a large public limited company and satisficing to a family-owned private limited company. Select and apply aims and objectives to reflect the situation of the business.

4 Primary and secondary objectives

Primary objectives are those which must be achieved if the business is to survive and be successful. These normally relate to issues such as **profit levels** and **market share**.

Secondary objectives tend to measure the efficiency of the organisation. They may affect the chances of success, but only in the long term. Examples include **customer care**, **administrative efficiency** and **labour turnover rates**.

Note: in recent years, customer care has assumed greater importance within many businesses. This has meant that improvements in this area have been reclassified as a primary objective.

Examiner's tip

This issue is relevant when answering a range of questions relating to the actions of a company. A useful line of evaluation might be to say that a business's response in any particular situation might depend, to some degree, upon the objectives that it pursues.

- **Private limited companies.** These are normally much smaller than public limited companies. Share capital must not exceed £50,000 and 'Ltd' must be included after the company's name. The shares of a private limited company cannot be bought and sold without the agreement of other shareholders. This, and the fact that the company cannot be listed on the Stock Exchange, means that private limited companies are likely to remain small.
- **Public limited companies.** The shares of these companies can be sold on the Stock Exchange and purchased by any business or individual. Public limited companies must be registered as public companies and have the term 'plc' after their name. They must have a minimum capital of £50,000 by law; in practice, this figure is likely to be far higher. Public limited companies have to publish more details of their financial affairs than private limited companies.
- **Cooperatives.** These are owned by workers or customers. Retail co-ops (owned by their customers) are common in the UK but have been in decline for many years. Cooperative societies are based on the principle of self-help. As with companies, people buy shares in cooperatives. The difference is that members of cooperatives have only one vote irrespective of the number of shares owned.
- **Mutuals (or non-profit-making organisations).** Insurance companies and building societies are examples of this form of business, in spite of high-profile demutualisations such as Norwich Union. Mutual organisations have no owners and they aim to provide the best possible service to their members (customers). Any surpluses earned are put back into the businesses.

1.1b Non-corporate businesses

Non-corporate businesses and their owners are not treated as separate entities — all an owner's private possessions can be sold to settle the business's debts in the event of bankruptcy. Sole traders and partners are usually said to have **unlimited liability**.

The different types of non-corporate business are as follows:
- **Sole traders or proprietors.** These are businesses owned by a single person, though the business may have a number of employees. Such one-person businesses are common in retailing and services such as plumbing and hairdressing.
- **Partnerships.** These comprise between 2 and 20 people who contribute capital and expertise to a business. The Partnership Act of 1890 established the legal rules under which partnerships operate. A partnership is usually based upon a **Deed of Partnership**, which sets out how much capital each partner has contributed, the share of profits each partner shall receive and the rules for electing new partners. Some partners may be 'sleeping partners', contributing capital but taking no active part in the operation of the business. Partnerships are common in the professions: for example, solicitors, dentists and accountants.

1.2 Forming a company

Those forming a company must send two main documents to the **Registrar of Companies**:
- **Memorandum of Association.** This sets out details of the company's name and address and its objectives in trading.
- **Articles of Association.** This details the internal arrangements of the company, including frequency of shareholders' meetings and distribution of profits.

Once these documents have been approved, the company receives a **Certificate of Incorporation** and can commence trading.

The advantages and disadvantages of the various legal forms of business are shown in Table 6.5.

Type of business	Advantages	Disadvantages
Sole traders	They are simple and cheap to establish, with few legal formalities. The owner receives all the profits (if there are any). They are able to respond quickly to changes in the market. Confidentiality is maintained, as financial details do not have to be published.	The owner is likely to be short of capital for investment and expansion. They have few assets as collateral to support applications for loans. Unlimited liability. It can be difficult for sole traders to take holidays.
Partnerships	Between them, partners may have a wide range of skills and knowledge. Partners are able to raise greater amounts of capital than sole traders. The pressure on owners is reduced as cover is available for holidays and decisions are made jointly.	Control is shared among the partners. Arguments are common among partners. There is still an absolute shortage of capital — even 20 people can only raise so much. Unlimited liability.
Private limited companies	Shareholders benefit from limited liability. Companies have access to greater amounts of capital. Private companies are required to divulge only a limited amount of financial information. Companies have a separate legal identity.	Private limited companies cannot sell their shares on the Stock Exchange. The need for permission to sell shares limits the potential for flexibility and growth. Limited companies have to conform to a number of expensive administrative formalities.
Public limited companies	They can gain positive publicity as a result of trading on the Stock Exchange. Stock Exchange quotation offers access to large amounts of capital. Suppliers are more willing to offer credit to public companies.	A Stock Exchange listing means emphasis is placed on short-term financial results, not long-term performance. Public companies are required to publish a great deal of financial information. Trading as a plc can result in hefty administrative expenses.
Cooperatives	Members (employees or customers) share in the success of the enterprise. The UK government and European Commission offer financial support to cooperatives.	Cooperatives suffer from a shortage of capital. They have a poor public image — often due to lack of funds.

Table 6.5 The advantages and disadvantages of different legal forms of business

Ideas for application

The legal form of the business provides considerable evidence for application. If the business is a plc, it has greater access to capital and more responsibility to publish financial information. The situation is quite different for a partnership. Make sure you use this information when developing arguments.

1.3 The divorce of ownership from control

Shareholders own companies, but directors and managers take day-to-day decisions. Many shareholders know little of the operation of the business, and the annual general meeting (AGM) does not provide a genuine opportunity to gain understanding of the business. This division between those who own the company and those who run it can result in decisions being taken which are not in the best interests of the owners. For example, managers may decide to pursue a policy of takeovers (to enhance their personal prestige); these takeovers may not prove to be in the best interests of shareholders.

2 Identifying business opportunities

Business opportunities can take a number of forms:

- **Turning an invention into a commercial opportunity.** Famous inventors, such as Sir Clive Sinclair, have attempted to turn their ideas into profitable products.
- **Purchasing a franchise.** Purchasing a franchise means buying a complete business idea from someone else. This reduces risk, especially if the business is well known (e.g. McDonald's). However, purchasing a franchise from a famous company can be very expensive and success (while more likely) is not guaranteed.
- **Finding a gap in the market.** This is more likely to succeed, as it is market orientated and considers the needs of customers. However, a gap may exist because it cannot be filled profitably. Success in these markets may attract rivals.

> **Examiner's tip**
>
> There are obvious links here with marketing. Some businesses continue to be product orientated, focusing on R&D and new products rather than consumers' needs. Such an approach has many dangers.

If a business succeeds in developing an idea or product, it is essential to protect it. A number of **forms of protection** exist:

- **Patents.** These provide the holders with an exclusive right to use an invention for a period of up to 20 years.
- **Trademarks.** These normally take the form of symbols, words or a combination of both. They are indicated by the symbol ® and allow a business to differentiate itself from competitors.
- **Registered designs.** This form of protection is available from the Designs Registry in London and operates for periods of up to 15 years.

Firms are keen to ensure that the results of (often expensive) research and development are protected from exploitation by rivals.

3 The problems of starting a new business

Over 30% of small businesses do not survive their first 3 years of trading. There are a number of reasons why such businesses fail.

3.1 Lack of effective market research

This is one of the most common causes of business failure. Entrepreneurs are often enthusiastic about their business idea and assume that the general public will be too.

Those starting a small business can conduct cheap and effective market research by:
- identifying a potential target market
- assessing likely competitors
- conducting limited primary research through interviews with possible customers
- deciding upon affordable media (local newspapers) through which to target potential customers

3.2 Lack of the necessary skills to run a business

Running a small business is demanding. Besides having knowledge of their product or service, entrepreneurs need to know about marketing, bookkeeping, purchasing, employment law, writing business plans, etc. Carrying out all the necessary duties involved can entail long hours and few holidays. For some entrepreneurs, the stress and workload of running a business proves too much.

3.3 Failing to turn ideas into a profitable product or service

About 80% of new products fail. Often the products stem from good ideas but are not marketed well, perhaps due to lack of finance. Even if an entrepreneur comes up with a good idea, he or she is likely to need advice and financial support in order to turn the concept into a commercial success.

3.4 Finance

This is an ongoing difficulty faced by many small businesses. Possible sources of start-up finances are listed in Table 6.6.

Possible sources of start-up finance	Comments
Redundancy pay and savings	A useful and relatively cheap source of finance, but rarely sufficient to establish a business in the marketplace.
Bank loans	A major source of finance for many new businesses, but loans can be expensive to reflect the degree of risk. Banks may also demand collateral for a loan or be unprepared to lend to high-risk businesses.
Venture capital	Small businesses can receive start-up capital from venture capitalists, but some providers are unwilling to lend more than £250,000 or to lend to new businesses.
Business angels	These are individuals who have sufficient personal funds to finance business start-ups. Although a new form of finance for business entrepreneurs, they are reputed to control in excess of £2 billion and most are prepared to advance sums under £50,000.
Government sources	These include sources such as the loan guarantee scheme. This scheme promises any bank advancing a loan to a new business that if the business fails to repay, the government will repay up to 80% of the loan.

Table 6.6 Sources of start-up finance for business

In spite of the range of sources outlined in Table 6.6, businesses still encounter many difficulties in raising the necessary funds. Potential creditors may be put off by:
- the high level of risk involved in making loans to new businesses
- the lack of financial planning (especially of cash flow) conducted by the entrepreneur

Ideas for application
SWOT analysis is much easier for a small business to conduct than a large one. The senior manager of a small business is likely to have an in-depth understanding of the business and the environment it inhabits. This is considerably more difficult for a multinational, in which case SWOT may be difficult, time consuming and possibly less appropriate.

A2 Objectives and strategy

This section builds upon the material covered at AS. It is recommended that you re-read the AS materials alongside those that follow. Although A2 questions will focus on the following topics, it is likely that some of the principles covered at AS will be needed to support your answers.

A Growing a business

1 Financing growth

Increasing the size of a business inevitably requires access to further capital to purchase the assets necessary to increase the scale of production. A number of internal and external sources of finance exist, as outlined below.

1.1 External sources of finance

- **Bank overdraft.** This is relatively cheap and easy to obtain, but repayable on demand. It allows a business to meet its short-term commitments, and the business only pays interest on the amount and for the period during which it is overdrawn.
- **Short-term loans.** These are given for specific purposes rather than just for use as working capital. Since interest is charged on the whole amount borrowed, they are usually more expensive than overdrafts.
- **Medium-term loans.** These are usually obtained from high-street banks, but can also be raised from specialist investment companies such as 3i. They can be repaid in instalments over the agreed period or by a one-off sum on an agreed date. The interest rate charged can be fixed or variable.
- **Long-term loans.** These are normally used to purchase capital assets such as buildings or other businesses that have a long life. Long-term loans usually have a fixed rate of interest attached and are given only after an independent survey of the asset has been completed. In addition, a comprehensive report on the business's past and expected performance is compiled. A mortgage loan is one that is usually secured on land or buildings for periods of 20 years or longer.
- **Leasing.** This is a form of finance whereby an asset is purchased by another organisation that then leases it to the user at an agreed rental. The lessor (the person or organisation leasing the asset) retains ownership. However, the cost to the lessee can be much lower than the equivalent cost of purchasing the asset outright. Another advantage of this form of acquiring equipment is that the lessor usually pays for all

maintenance costs. Leasing is particularly advantageous for companies in high-technology industries.

- **Debentures.** Only very large and established companies usually issue debentures and these can be sold to insurance companies, pension funds, etc. Debentures can only be issued to members of the public by public limited companies.
- **Issuing shares.** An established business may be able to issue further shares to its existing shareholders at a favourable rate in order to obtain more funds. Alternatively, if the company is a plc, it can place the shares with a financial institution for it to sell, or shares can be traded directly on the Stock Exchange.
- **Venture capital providers.** These offer financial support to high-risk projects that might be judged too risky by institutions such as high-street banks. Venture capital is usually in the form of a loans-and-shares package and is unlikely to exceed £250,000.

1.2 Internal sources of finance

- **The sale of assets.** Assets such as property and buildings may be unwanted and can be sold to raise capital. Alternatively, such assets can be sold and leased back. The Kingfisher Group (which owns Woolworth's and many other retailers) has used this technique to raise large sums of money.
- **Retained profit.** This is a major source of finance for all types of business, including those aiming to expand. About 70% of investment is from this source and it offers relatively cheap funding. The disadvantage of using retained profits in this way is that dividends paid to shareholders may suffer.
- **Working capital.** This can be a source of relatively small amounts of finance. Through techniques such as limiting credit offered, insisting on prompt payment by debtors and reducing stock levels, businesses can 'free up' funds for long-term investment.

Examiner's tip

It is important to match the source of finance to the type of business, its circumstances and its degree of success. Selecting (and justifying) an appropriate source of finance as part of an answer is an evaluative skill which is likely to attract high marks if completed successfully.

2 Financial problems accompanying business growth

2.1 Overtrading

This occurs when a business expands too quickly and with too little financial planning. As a consequence, it may find itself short of working capital and may even be forced into liquidation should a creditor demand early payment of debts. Overtrading is common among businesses that are growing rapidly, especially if the growth is unexpected. The solution is to arrange long-term finance in advance in order to ensure that the business has sufficient funds to meet short-term financial commitments.

2.2 Cash-flow difficulties

A period of growth, particularly a prolonged period, is likely to impose a strain on a business's cash flow. Firms win new markets by offering favourable credit terms to attract new customers. The result might be a large order, possibly at a favourable price, but with no inflow of money for some time. Meanwhile, the costs of raw materials and labour have to be met. The situation can deteriorate as new suppliers demand immediate

Advantages	Disadvantages
For the seller there is a benefit in selling what may be a loss-making activity.	Many management buyouts fail within a few years because the business is fundamentally unprofitable.
A successful buyout may lead to the business's flotation on the Stock Exchange and great wealth for the management team.	Management buyouts are often accompanied by rationalisation and job losses as the firm attempts to improve financial performance.
The buyers have the challenge and enjoyment of running their own business.	Management buyouts frequently have limited access to capital and this can hinder their performance.
A management buyout may result in jobs being saved, as the alternative might have been closure.	

Table 6.8 Advantages and disadvantages of management buyouts

Management buyouts can be funded in a variety of ways:

- Members of the management team are likely to contribute funds from their own personal wealth, perhaps by remortgaging their properties.
- Merchant banks or venture capital specialists may provide finance.
- Some management buyouts are financed in part by selling shares to employees (offering them the chance to benefit from any future profits).

Examiner's tip

When assessing management buyouts, remember to consider the potential effects upon all groups that are party to the change of ownership. A balanced response will take into account the needs of the workforce, the local community and the business's customers as well as the new management team.

Ideas for application

Increasing scale is an attractive proposition for businesses that incur high levels of fixed costs. Merging with, or taking over, a similar business can assist in reducing costs per unit and increasing competitiveness.

B Business strategy

Strategy is a medium- to long-term plan designed to assist a business in achieving its objectives. Strategy entails taking decisions that are likely to have significant long-term effects on the business. It is normally planned and implemented by senior managers. For example, the decision by Lloyds TSB Group to purchase Scottish Widows Mutual Assurance Society would have been taken at a senior management level.

1 Strategic planning techniques

A number of techniques exist to assist managers in planning and executing strategy.

1.1 Ansoff's matrix

This **product–market matrix** (see Figure 6.4) assists businesses in evaluating the organisation and the market in which it operates. Developed by Igor Ansoff in 1957, it represents a useful framework for considering the relationship between marketing and overall strategy. The technique considers product and market growth and analyses the degree of risk attached to the range of options open to the business. Key findings of Ansoff's matrix include the following:

- Staying with what you know (e.g. market penetration) represents relatively little risk.
- Moving into new markets with new products is a high-risk strategy.
- Assessment is made of the value of each option.

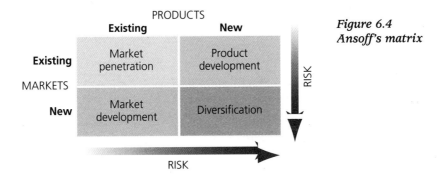

Figure 6.4
Ansoff's matrix

1.2 Decision trees

Strategic management is made easier by **reducing uncertainty** in decision making. Alternatively, senior managers might seek **to measure the degree of uncertainty involved in a decision** and take it into account. Uncertainty can be measured by probability, and the calculation of probability can be used to assess the extent of uncertainty in any decision.

Central to the use of decision trees is the calculation of the expected value of each aspect of a particular decision. Businesses can calculate the expected value of an outcome by multiplying the probability of that outcome by the benefit that the business can expect if it happens.

Example

A business is considering whether or not to launch a new product. If it does so and the product succeeds, the business forecasts £1.6 million profits. The product has a 0.25 (25%) probability of success. The expected value from the new product will be:

£1.6 million × 0.25 = £400,000

Decision trees can be used to represent and offer some evaluation of the choices open to a business. **There are various stages in constructing a decision tree**:

(1) Identify the options available to the business.

(2) Assess the likely outcomes of each of these actions.

(3) Attach probabilities to each possibility available to the firm.

(4) Estimate the likely financial returns from each course of action identified.

(5) Calculate the expected value of each course of action.

(6) Choose the course of action generating the highest expected value.

In decision trees, as shown in Figure 6.5:
- A decision point is indicated by a square.
- Circles represent alternatives with probabilities attached.
- The probabilities of each event taking place are shown by decimal figures on the appropriate line.
- Any costs associated with decisions are shown next to the decision and preceded by a minus sign.
- The benefits of outcomes are listed on the right-hand side of the decision tree.

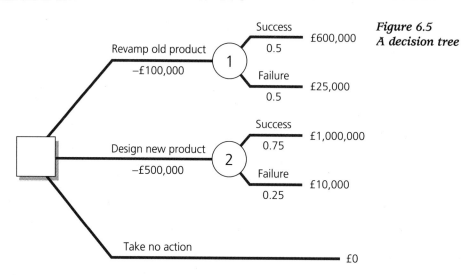

Figure 6.5
A decision tree

The outcomes for the choices available to the business in Figure 6.5 are as follows:
- Revamp old product = (0.5 × £600,000) + (0.5 × £25,000) − £100,000 = £212,500
- Design new product = (0.75 × £1,000,000) + (0.25 × £10,000) − £500,000 = £252,500
- Do nothing = £0

Given the anticipated probabilities and the forecast revenues and costs, a logical choice in these circumstances would be to design a new product.

The advantages and disadvantages of using decision trees are given in Table 6.9.

Advantages	Disadvantages
Encourage a logical approach to decision making by businesses and consideration of all possibilities.	It is very difficult to get accurate data, especially relating to probabilities.
Especially useful in circumstances where accurate values can be attached to options.	Management bias can be introduced into the data to achieve a desired decision.
Help businesses to take risk into account when taking decisions.	Change (particularly in the business environment) may affect the accuracy of the decision.
Discourage instinctive decisions or use of 'gut reactions'.	

Table 6.9 Advantages and disadvantages of decision trees

Examiner's tip

Decision trees should be calculated by working from right to left. You should always show all your workings in case of error and ensure that you do not forget to deduct any costs associated with a particular course of action.

1.3 Porter's strategic matrix

Michael Porter of the Harvard Business School is one of the foremost business writers in the world today. One of his best-known contributions to management thinking is his strategic matrix (Figure 6.6). Its purpose is to assist managers in assessing strategy. It assesses whether the business is aiming at producing low-cost or differentiated products. Simultaneously, it judges whether the business is operating in a niche or a mass market.

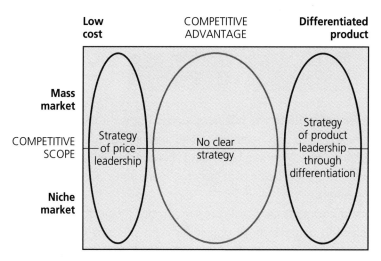

Figure 6.6 Porter's strategic matrix

The fundamental point of Porter's theory is that, whether operating in a niche or a mass market, a business should aim to be either a low-cost producer or to sell a product that is highly differentiated from those of rivals. It should not allow its strategy to drift towards the middle of the matrix, not seeking price or product leadership.

A number of airlines have pursued very successful strategies based on price leadership. Arguably the most successful has been Ryan Air. At the same time, British Airways has not operated a clear strategy which may, in part, explain the problems that the company has encountered over recent years.

Examiner's tip

Many questions focus on business strategy. Porter's strategic matrix is a useful tool to assess the quality of management strategic planning. In particular, it can be used as a framework to compare two alternative strategies.

2 Corporate or strategic plans

Strategic planning involves **matching the corporate objectives to the resources available**. The corporate plan is therefore the strategic process of allocating resources within an organisation in order to achieve its strategic or corporate aims. Corporate plans represent a business's strategy.

A number of factors may influence senior managers in constructing their corporate or strategic plans (see Figure 6.7):
- **The organisation's mission statement.** If, for example, this makes reference to becoming market leader, then the associated corporate plan will address issues such as quality, customer service and, perhaps, takeovers.

Figure 6.7
Corporate objectives,
strategy and associated
influences

- **The resources available to the business.** Grand plans for expansion may founder if a business has access to only relatively small amounts of finance. Similarly, improving customer service may require greater (and more highly skilled) human resources than those available to the business at present. Strategies are normally based upon a business's strengths.
- **The actions of competitors**. Managers set corporate objectives and plan their associated strategies to achieve these objectives with the aim of operating in profitable markets. Actions of competitors (e.g. a competitor brings out a new and revolutionary product) can affect the profitability of markets and in turn have knock-on effects on corporate objectives.

It is normal for strategic plans to be determined and operated by senior managers within the business. However, some business analysts (for example, Tom Peters) have argued that autonomous workgroups should contribute to the generation of corporate plans. Over recent years, large companies, such as British Airways, have introduced staff training with the aim of reinforcing company values and encouraging all staff to contribute to the achievement of corporate objectives.

> **Examiner's tip**
> It is important to be clear about the terminology in this area of the specification. Corporate or strategic objectives are the goals of the whole organisation. Strategy in this context relates to the plan that is necessary to achieve the objectives.

3 *Contingency planning*

All plans, and especially long-term ones, can go wrong. Businesses should prepare for this and also for the unexpected. In such circumstances, a business may put a contingency plan into operation.

3.1 Circumstances requiring a contingency plan

There are a number of circumstances in which the implementation of a contingency plan is required:
- **During a sudden slump in demand.** This was experienced by the aircraft manufacturer Boeing following the attack on the World Trade Center in New York in September 2001.
- **When a business becomes the object of the attentions of a pressure group.** For

example, Monsanto was subject to a great deal of criticism following its involvement in the development of genetically modified crops. The company attracted a great deal of adverse publicity before announcing a major change of strategy.

- **When a new and highly efficient competitor emerges.** For example, Hoover's sales of vacuum cleaners suffered as a result of the emergence of Dyson as a rival.

3.2 Features of a contingency plan

Contingency plans should contain a number of common elements:

- an **identified team headed by an experienced manager** to assume control in the event of a crisis
- **sufficient resources** to deal with the problem — the crisis team will need financial resources, communications technology and access to experts in order to cope with the unexpected
- **effective communications systems** that can identify the nature and causes of the problem as well as prepare appropriate responses
- **efficient links with the media**, as ill-informed speculation can be very damaging to the organisation

Contingency plans need to be reviewed regularly to ensure that they are relevant and up to date. It may be necessary to test the effectiveness of contingency plans and systems by simulating a crisis and practising the planned response.

Specification checklist and revision progress chart

To use this chart you should first make sure that you know which awarding body (AQA, Edexcel or OCR) sets your examinations. Then use the appropriate column from the chart. The book has been structured to mirror the way in which AQA has organised its business studies subject content into AS and A2 sections. Thus if you are an AQA student, you should just use the book as it is; the AS section will cover all the topics you need for these examinations and the same for A2. However, Edexcel and OCR have made minor differences in the ways in which the topics have been divided up.

You need to check precisely what is included in AS and A2 using the chart below to make sure your revision is complete. A tick (✔) indicates that a topic is included within the AS or A2 specification as set out in this book. A cross (✗) shows that a topic is not included. If it is included elsewhere, a brief explanation is given.

AS Marketing	AQA	Edexcel	OCR	Revision completed
Segmentation analysis	✔	✔	✔	
Market share size and growth	✔	✔	✔	
Market research	✔	✔	✔	
Confidence levels	✔	✗	✗	
Marketing objectives	✔	✔	✔	
Niche and mass marketing	✔	Not explicitly stated	✔	
Product life cycle	✔	✔	✔	
Product portfolio analysis	✔	✔	✔	
USP and adding value	✔	✔	✗	
The marketing mix	✔	✔	✔	
Product design and development	✔	A2 topic	✔	
Pricing: strategies, methods and tactics	✔	✔	Limited coverage at AS — more at A2	
Promotion: types	✔	✔	✔	
Place: distribution targets and channels	✔	✔	Only distribution channels	
Price elasticity	✔	✔	✔	
Income elasticity	✔	✔	✗	
		Edexcel includes cross elasticity too.		

AS Accounting and Finance	AQA	Edexcel	OCR	Revision completed
Costs: fixed, variable, direct, indirect	✔	✔	✔	
Revenue, costs and profit	✔	✔	✔	
Break-even and contribution	✔	✔	✔	
Cash-flow management	✔	✔	✔	
Cash flow v. profit	✔	✔	✔	

AS Accounting and Finance (continued)	AQA	Edexcel	OCR	Revision completed
Budgets	✔	✔	✔	
Variance analysis	✔	✔	✔	
Cost and profit centres	✔	A2 topic	A2 topic	
		NB: Edexcel includes depreciation, an introduction to balance sheets, profit and loss accounts and ratio analysis at AS.	NB: some investment appraisal (payback and ARR) as well as balance sheets and profit and loss accounts are also part of AS.	

AS People and Organisations	AQA	Edexcel	OCR	Revision completed
Organisational structure	✔	✔	✔	
Management by objectives	✔	✗	✗	
Delegation and consultation	✔	✔	A2 topic	
Motivation theory	✔	✔	✔	
Motivation in practice	✔	✔	✔	
Financial incentives	✔	A2 topic	✔	
Leadership and management styles	✔	✔	✔	
HRM: workforce planning	✔	A2 topic	✔	
HRM: recruitment and training	✔	A2 topic	✔	
		Communication is an AS topic for Edexcel.		

AS Operations Management	AQA	Edexcel	OCR	Revision completed
Economies and diseconomies of scale	✔	✔	✔	
Capacity utilisation	✔	✔	✔	
Capital and labour intensity	✔	✔	✔	
Stock control	✔	✔	✔	
Quality control and assurance	✔	✔	✔	
Cell production	✔	✔	✔	
Just-in-time	✔	✔	✔	
Time-based management	✔	Not explicitly stated	✗	
Kaizen	✔	Not explicitly stated	✔	

AS External Influences	AQA	Edexcel	OCR	Revision completed
Markets and competition	✔	✔	✔	
The business cycle	✔	A2 topic	✔	
Interest rates	✔	✔	✔	
Exchange rates	✔	✔	✔	
Inflation and unemployment	✔	✔	✔	
Business law	✔	✔	✔	
Social responsibilities	✔	✔	✔	
Business ethics	✔	A2 topic	A2 topic	
Technological change	✔	A2 topic	✔	

AS Objectives and Strategy	AQA	Edexcel	OCR	Revision completed
Starting a small business	✔	A2 topic	✔	
Identifying business opportunities	✔	✗	✔	
Legal structure of businesses	✔	✔	✔	
Problems of business start-ups	✔	A2 topic	✗	
Corporate aims and goals	✔	✔	✔	
Stakeholders' aims and objectives	✔	✔	✔	
SWOT analysis	✔	A2 topic	✔	
			NB: also includes measuring business size.	

A2 Marketing	AQA	Edexcel	OCR	Revision completed
Asset- and market-led marketing	✔	AS topic	AS topic	
Trend analysis, moving averages	✔	✔	✔	
Extrapolation and correlation	✔	✔	✔	
Marketing models	✔	✔	✔	
Co-ordinating marketing and other functions	✔	✔	AS topic	
Marketing budgets	✔	Not explicitly stated	✗	
Sales forecasting	✔	✔	✔	
		NB: also includes scatter graphs and line of best fit.	NB: also includes standard deviation, normal distribution and sampling methods.	

A2 Accounting and Finance	AQA	Edexcel	OCR	Revision completed
Capital and revenue expenditure	✔	AS topic	✔	
Profit and loss accounts	✔	✔	✔	
Balance sheets	✔	✔	✔	
Working capital	✔	✔	✔	
Depreciation	✔	AS topic	✔	
Window-dressing accounts	✔	✗	✔	
Ratio analysis	✔	✔	✔	
Complex break-even, special order decisions	✔	✔	✔	
Quantitative investment appraisal	✔	✔	AS topic	
Qualitative investment appraisal	✔	✔	AS topic	
		NB: much basic material on accounts and ratio analysis is covered at AS.	NB: module includes section on accounting concepts and methods of costing.	

A2 People in Organisations	AQA	Edexcel	OCR	Revision completed
Communication: importance	✔	AS topic	✔	
Communication: difficulties and solutions	✔	AS topic	✔	
Individual and collective bargaining	✔	✔	✔	
Trade unions, ACAS disputes and methods of resolution	✔	✔	✔	
Employee participation and industrial democracy	✔	✔	✔	
Employment law	✔	✔	✔	
HRM: integrated workforce planning	✔	✔	AS topic	
HRM and financial incentives	✔	✔	AS topic	
Personnel performance indicators	✔	✗	✗	
		NB: job specifications and descriptions and selection are part of A2 for Edexcel.	NB: also includes a section on the management of change.	

A2 Operations Management	AQA	Edexcel	OCR	Revision completed
Research and development	✔	✔	✔	
Critical path analysis	✔	✔	In A2 Objectives and Strategy	
IT within organisations	✔	✔	✔	
Location: regional and international	✔	Edexcel includes a section on pros and cons of multinationals.	✔	
			NB: includes material on costs, costing methods and break-even as well as material on productive efficiency covered at AS.	

A2 External Influences	AQA	Edexcel	OCR	Revision completed
Economic factors and business strategy	✔	✔	✔	
International competitiveness	✔	✔	✔	
Economic growth and business	✔	✔	✔	
EU and emerging markets	✔	✔	✔	
Monetary and fiscal policy	✔	✔	✔	
Intervention v. laissez faire	✔	AS topic	✔	
Social responsibilities	✔	✔	✔	
Social audits	✔	✔ Environmental audits too	✔	

A2 External Influences (continued)	AQA	Edexcel	OCR	Revision completed
Business ethics	✔	✔	✔	
Environmental pressures and opportunities	✔	✔	✔	
Pressure groups	✔	✔	✔	
Political change	✔	✔ A major section on managing change	✔	

A2 Objectives and Strategy	AQA	Edexcel	OCR	Revision completed
Mission statements	✔	AS topic	✔	
Organisational culture	✔	✔	✔	
Financing growth	✔	✔	✔	
Management reorganisation and growth	✔	✔	✔	
Problems of changing size	✔	✔	✔	
Changes in business ownership	✔	✔	✔	
Decision-making models (e.g. Ansoff)	✔	✔	✔	
Decision trees	✔	✔	✔	
Corporate plans	✔	✔	✔	
Contingency planning	✔	Not explicitly stated	✔	
			This module integrates much of the material studied at AS and A2.	